Stop Stealing Sheep

Stop Stealing Sheep

& find out how type works

Second Edition

Erik Spiekermann
& E.M.Ginger

Adobe Press
Berkeley, California

Stop Stealing Sheep & find out how type works
Second Edition
E RIK S PIEKERMANN AND E.M. G INGER

Copyright © 2003 Adobe Systems Incorporated.
All rights reserved.

This Adobe Press book is published by
Peachpit Press.

Peachpit Press is a division of Pearson Education.

For more information on Adobe Press books,
contact:
> Peachpit Press
> 1249 Eighth St.
> Berkeley, California 94710
> 510-524-2178 (tel)
> 510-524-2221 (fax)
> http://www.peachpit.com

To report errors, please send a note to
errata@peachpit.com

ISBN: 0-201-70339-4

10 9 8 7 6 5 4 3 2 1

Printed and bound
in the United States of America.

5

Stealing Sheep? Letterspacing lower case? Professionals in all trades, whether they be dentists, carpenters, or nuclear scientists, communicate in languages that seem secretive and incomprehensible to outsiders; type designers and typographers are no exception. Typographic terminology sounds cryptic enough to put off anyone but the most hard-nosed typomaniac. The aim of this book is to clarify the language of typography for people who want to communicate more effectively with type.

These days people need better ways to communicate to more diverse audiences. We know from experience that what we have to say is much easier for others to understand if we put it in the right voice; type is that voice, the visible language linking writer and reader. With thousands of typefaces available, choosing the right one to express even the simplest idea is bewildering to most everyone but practiced professionals.

Familiar images are used in this book to show that typography is not an art for the chosen few, but a powerful tool for anyone who has something to say and needs to say it in print or on a screen. You will have ample opportunity to find out why there are so many typefaces, how they ought to be used, and why more of them are needed every day.

We see so much type that we sometimes stop looking. This is not necessarily a bad thing, as in the case of this sign, which tells us that we may not enter this street between eleven and six, nor between eleven and six, and certainly not between eleven and six.

The small picture here is from this book's first edition, printed in 1992. Since then, authorities in Stockholm have cleaned up the sign and modernized the hardware, but extended the no-go hours until 6 am. They haven't, however, changed their attitude.

This is a sidebar. As you can see by the small type, the copy here is not for the faint of heart, nor for the casual reader. All the information that might be a little heady for novices is these narrow columns; it is, however, right at hand when one becomes infected by one's first attacks of typomania.

For those who already know something about type and typography and who simply want to check some facts, read some gossip, and shake their heads at our opinionated comments, this is the space to watch.

In 1936, Frederic Goudy was in New York City to receive an award for excellence in type design. Upon accepting a certificate, he took one look at it and declared that "Anyone who would letterspace black letter would steal sheep." This was an uncomfortable moment for the man sitting in the audience who had hand lettered the award certificate. Mr. Goudy later apologized profusely, claiming that he said that about everything.

You might have noticed that our book cover reads "lower case," while here it reads "black letter" – two very different things. Lower case letters, as opposed to CAPITAL LETTERS, are what you are now reading; black letter isn't seen very often and looks like this.

We're not sure how "black letter" in this anecdote got changed to "lower case," but we've always known it to be the latter; whichever way, it makes infinite sense. By the time you finish this book we hope you will understand and be amused by Mr. Goudy's pronouncement.

PAUL WATZLAWICK

You cannot *not* communicate.

Paul Watzlawick (1922–)
is author of *Pragmatics of
Human Communication*, a
book about the influence of
media on people's behavior.
"You cannot not communicate"
is known as Watzlawick's First
Axiom of Communication.

CHAPTER 1

Type is everywhere

Have you ever been to Japan? A friend who went there recently reported that he had never felt so lost in his life. Why? Because he could not read anything: not road signs, not price tags, not instructions of any kind. It made him feel stupid, he said. It also made him realize how much we all depend on written communication.

Picture yourself in a world without type. True, you could do without some of the ubiquitous advertising messages, but you wouldn't even know what the packages on your breakfast table contained.

Works in most languages, avoiding tasteless mistakes: *S* for Salt and *P* for Pepper.

Sure enough, there are pictures on them – grazing cows on a paper carton suggest that milk is inside, and cereal packaging has appetizing images to make you hungry. But pick up salt or pepper, and what do you look for? S and P!

Try to find your way around without type and you'll be as lost as most of us would be in Japan, where there is plenty of type to read, but only for those who have learned to read the right sort of characters.

You've hardly got your eyes open when you have to digest your first bite of type. How else would you know how much calcium fits on your spoon?

DIE ZEIT
WOCHENZEITUNG FÜR POLITIK · WIRTSCHAFT · HANDEL UND KULTUR
996, 51. Jahrgang
C 745

THE WALL STREET JOURNAL EUROP

© 1996 Dow Jones & Company, Inc. All Rights Reserved.

Frankfurter Allgemeine
ZEITUNG FÜR DEUTSCHLAND

INANCIAL TIME

Herald INTERNATIONAL Tribune
PUBLISHED WITH THE NEW YORK TIMES AND THE WASHINGTON POST

LE FIGARO
économie

Paris

Meri

Le Monde
Cahier
Initiatives-Métie

Russie : un général arbitre du second tour P. 23

VISIOCONFÉRENCE INTÉGRÉE
Les technologies les plus pointues
intégrées dans le mobilier d'auteur

La Tribune
collectonie

Breakfast for some people wouldn't be the same without the morning paper. And here it is again: inevitable type. Most people call it "print" and don't pay too much attention to typographic subtleties. You've probably never compared the small text typefaces in different newspapers, but you do know that some newspapers are easier to read than others. It might be because they have larger type, better pictures, and lots of headings to guide you through the stories. Regardless, all these differences are conveyed by type. In fact, a newspaper gets its look, its personality, from the typefaces used and the ways in which they are arranged on the page. We easily recognize our favorite newspapers on the newsstand, even if we only see the edge of a page, just as we recognize our friends by seeing only their hands or their hair. And just as people look different across the world, so do the newspapers in different countries. What looks totally unacceptable to a North American reader will please the French reader at breakfast, while an Italian might find a German daily paper too monotonous.

Type says much more about a newspaper than just the words it spells.

Of course, it's not only type or layout that distinguishes newspapers, it is also the combination of words. Some languages have lots of accents, like French; some have very long words, like Dutch or Finnish; and some use extremely short ones, as in a British tabloid. Not every typeface is suited for every language, which also explains why certain type styles are popular in certain countries but not necessarily anywhere else.

新案開倒團集海東
二約產資結凍
同取望可主華
ى فى مجتمعنا
كله وستدور بتكاتف
ات نون نسبة الزيادة ال

What appears frightfully complex and incomprehensible to people who can only read the Latin alphabet brings news to the majority of the world's population. Chinese and Arabic are spoken by more than half of the people on this planet.

áåæäàœöøçß¡¿

Some of the accents, special signs, and characters seen in languages other than English, giving each language its unique appearance.

A bargain that benefits everyon[e]

Larry Elliott

> According to the index, we could take a 0.6% pay cut and be just as well off this year as last

The strikes and pay disputes on the railways appear to have caught ministers by surprise. Rather complacently, they assumed that industrial unrest was what happened to previous Labour governments, not this one.

One body of officialdom that will have been shocked is at the Bank of England, where there has been concern for over a year that the tightness of the labour market would spill over into pressure for higher pay. The only surprise to the Bank is that it has taken so long.

For the past quarter a decade 10 years of uninterrupted growth in the UK, and in the south-east especially, where the main flashpoints are occurring, there are only a few islands of inner-city joblessness in a sea of full employment. Walk down any high street and the windows of shops, restaurants and pubs will have signs saying that they are in a very comfortable position. Inflation may be low but it in other ways the region shows the classic signs of overheating: rising prices, acute shortages of labour. The skilled are wanted by bars, restaurants and shops, where business is booming as a result of strong consumer demand, while the extra money being pumped into health and education means that the public sector is also competing for a shrinking pool of workers.

On the railways, the outlook for employees is even brighter. The fragmentation of the network, the decision of operating companies to cut the number of drivers in order to boost profitability and the stiff penalties for franchises for delays and cancellations, mean that the conditions could hardly be better for the unions, which are seeking to improve the living standards of members. The pay deal being negotiated are good ones, but the fact is that most people in a job are doing well in the current climate.

Muscular impact

…for the earnings figures to show in February and March, reflecting the gargantuan size of City bonuses…

So what happens next?…

Hugh Osmond

larry.elliott@guardian.co.uk

Debate Andrew Mackenzie and David Rice

Companies can show the way to a more ethical wor[ld]

Globalisation has weakened a marginalised political individual, business is asked to fill the gaps. But it is being asked to lead the way towards a more ethical world without the authority or incentive to do so. Politicians need to become more confident about setting standards for business, based on an internationalist approach.

Briefing Charlotte Denny

Argentina sends IMF back to the drawing board

This brings us back to type and newspapers. What might look quite obvious and normal to you when you read your daily paper is the result of careful planning and applied craft. Even newspapers with pages that look messy are laid out following complex grids and strict hierarchies.

The artistry comes in offering the information in such a way that the reader doesn't get sidetracked into thinking about the fact that someone had to carefully prepare every line, paragraph, and column into structured pages. Design – in this case at least – has to be invisible. Typefaces used for these hardworking tasks are therefore by definition "invisible." They have to look so normal that you don't even notice you're reading them. And this is exactly why designing type is such an obscure profession; who thinks about people who produce invisible things? Nevertheless, every walk of life is defined by, expressed with and, indeed dependent on type and typography.

The Guardian, one of Britain's leading newspapers, is designed to a grid.

More and more people read the news not on paper, but on TV screens or computer monitors. Type and layout have to be reconsidered for these applications.

Just as the newspaper on the opposite page is laid out according to an underlying structure of some intricacy, this book is designed within its own constraints.

The page is divided into equal parts, each of which has the same proportion as the whole page, i.e., 2:3. The page is made up of 144 rectangles, each one measuring 12 by 18 millimeters, 12 rectangles across and 12 down. This makes the page 144 by 216 millimeters, or roughly 5 $^{21}/_{32}$ by 8 ½ inches. The columns are multiples of the 12-millimeter unit. Because there has to be some distance between columns, 3 mm (or more for wider columns) have to be subtracted from these multiples of 12 to arrive at the proper column width.

The distance between lines of type (still archaically referred to as *leading* – rhymes with *heading*) is measured in multiples of 1.5 mm. All typographic elements are positioned on this baseline grid of 1.5 mm, which is fine enough to be all but invisible to the reader, but which helps layout and production. The discipline offered by this kind of fine grid gives the same sort of coherence to a page as bricks do to a building. They are small enough to allow for all styles of architecture, while serving as the common denominator for all other proportions.

If you think that the choice of a typeface is something of little importance because nobody would know the difference anyway, you'll be surprised to hear that experts spend an enormous amount of time and effort perfecting details that are unseen by the untrained eye.

It is a bit like having been to a concert, thoroughly enjoying it, then reading in the paper the next morning that the conductor had been incompetent, the orchestra out of tune, and the piece of music not worth performing in the first place. While you had a great night out, some experts were unhappy with the performance because their standards and expectations were different than yours.

The same thing happens when you have a glass of wine. While you might be perfectly happy with whatever you're drinking, someone at the table will make a face and go on at length about why this particular bottle is too warm, how that year wasn't very good, and that he just happens to have a case full of some amazing stuff at home that the uncle of a friend imports directly from France.

Does that make you a fool or does it simply say that there are varying levels of quality and satisfaction in everything we do?

Food and design: how often do we buy the typographic promise without knowing much about the product? Stereotypes abound – some colors suggest certain foods, particular typefaces suggest different flavors and qualities. Without these unwritten rules we wouldn't know what to buy or order.

JEDEM
DAS SEINE

SUUM CUIQUE

Chacun à son goût

As they say in England: "Different strokes for different folks."

The kinds of food and drink known to mankind are almost limitless. No single person could be expected to know them all. One guide through this maze of taste and nourishment, of sustenance as well as gluttony, is offered by the labels on products; as long as they are packaged in containers that can carry information. Without typography we wouldn't know which contains what or what should be used which way.

Small wonder that type on food packages is often hand lettered, because standard typefaces don't seem to be able to express this vast array of tastes and promises. Hand lettering these days sometimes means using software programs, such as Adobe Illustrator, that combine design and artwork at a level unimaginable only a decade ago. Anything a graphic designer can think of can be produced in amazing quality.

Effects that mimic hand lettering, stone carving, sewing, or etching are all easily achieved electronically.

2002

Department of Fontography
Adobe Type Library

nstructions for Form TYPE4U
2. Can Add Emphasis To Words Through Type
(With help from Adobe Type Library)

otice of History

en Gutenberg printed his forty-two-line Bible in 1456, he had only one typeface
ce: the formal, square-text Gothic letter that mimicked the lettering of scribes. Who could have
gined typography would become so rich a resource for communication.

y, designers and desktop publishers have tens of thousands of typefaces to choose from, and new
ns are added continuously. To help make the job of selecting type easier, we have organized Adobe
aces according to a simplified classification system. It is based on the internationally recognized
m that has been adopted by the Association Typographique Internationale (ATypl), an organization
ets standards for the typographic industry. The British Standards Institution and the American
nal Standards Institute also have adopted this classification system.

Gutenberg printed his forty-two-line Bible in 1456, he had only one typeface
e: the formal, square-text Gothic letter that mimicked the lettering of scribes. Who
ed typography would become so rich as a resource for comm
p publishers have tens of thousands of t
ously. To help m

Store	iTools	iCards	QuickTime	Support	Mac OS X

Create Your Account   View Current Order   Software   Accessories   Help

Create your Apple ID.

◉ Complete the fields below, then click the Continue button to save.

Email address (this will be your new Apple ID)

Password (at least 6 characters)

First Name

Last Name

Daytime Phone *(optional)

Ext.

☑ Stay informed. We'll keep you up to date with Apple news, software updates, special offers, and information
about related products and services from other companies.

You're in control. You always have access to your personal information and contact preferences, so you can change
them at any time. To learn how Apple safeguards your personal information, please review the Apple Customer
Privacy Policy. If you would rather not receive this information, please uncheck the box above.

Continue

Chang
•When (
Bible in
choice: I
that mim
could ha
become i

•Today, d
have tens
from, and
continuous
selecting t
dobe typ
assificatio
ternationa
en adopt
pographic
ianization
ographic
itution an
ndards In
sification

en Guteni
in 1456,
e: the for
iimicked
have ima
e so rich
. designe
thousan
nd new c
ously. Tc
g type ea
ypefaces
ation sys
nally red
pted by
hique In
ion that

From
Of   Extension

☐ URGENT! ☐ RETURNED CALL ☐ CALL BACK WIL CAL AGA

REGISTERED NOTEPAD NO 1234567 89-0

WHILE YOU W

Date
1 To   Area code
From
Of   Extension

☐ URGENT! ☐ RETURNED CALL ☐ CALL BACK W C C

REGISTERED NOTEPAD NO 1234567 89-0

WHILE YOU W

Date
1 To   Area cod
From
Of   Extensio

☐ URGENT! ☐ RETURNED CALL ☐ CALL BACK

REGISTERED NOTEPAD NO 1234567 89-0

WHILE YOU W

Enter your information

Fields marked with an asterisk (*) are required. If you do not
provide the required information, you will not be able to complete
your registration or purchase transaction. By providing this
information, you agree that Adobe Systems Benelux, B.V.
("Adobe") may process the information for such purposes.

*First name

*Family/last name

Note : Your product(s) will be registered to the company you list
here. If you are purchasing or registering product(s) for personal
use, leave the next three fields blank.

Company

Job title

Department

*Street Address

Street Address Line 2

*City

*Zip/Postal Code

Country   AUSTRIA

Daytime Phone   Extension

*Email address

Fax number

Select Login and password

You will use your Login and password to
access and modify your registration and
account information

*Login

*Password   *Confirm password

Password hint (Must be different from
password)

☑ Remember my Login

Note : Your password must be at least four
characters long.

Uses of my information

☐ I would like to receive from Adobe,
either by email or regular mail,
information and special promotions on
Adobe software products and related
services.

☐ I would like to receive from parties
other than Adobe, who market
technology related products and
services, either by email or regular
mail, information and special promotions
on their products and services provided
such parties are located in the European
Union.

☐ *I agree that Adobe may process my
data to complete my purchase or
registration transaction.

☐ *Subject to the choices made above, I
agree to Adobe transferring my personal
information to Adobe affiliates, business
partners, and vendors outside of the
European Union, including the United
States, for the purpose of processing my
registration or order and otherwise for
the purposes set forth in the Adobe
Online Privacy Policy.

*If you are a resident of a member state of
the European Union, we cannot complete your
purchase or registration transaction unless
you check these boxes.

*Preferred contact method

ADDRESS   PHONE

STATE OF COLLEGE SALES TAX EXEMPTION CERTIFICATE

☐ Your Phone Number   ☐ Your Address (we cannot ship to P.O. Boxes)

DID YOU FORGET? Please check the followi

Order Form

The Beehive Company ©

P.O. Box 123
Nowheretown, CT 02361-5423

Please check your Address. We cannot ship to a P.O. Box

Ordered By:

Code: 234556
Sans Serif F. Rutiger
300 Rotis ST STE 8
New Jack City DC 92312-2345

*EXTENDED ORDERING HOURS
FROM 11/115 - 12/13!*

Mastercard	Qty	Description	Price Each	Total Price

Credit Card Orde

*Monday through
Saturdays 8 am*

FAX Orders: 1

Office use only

Phone Number:
Day ( )

Method of Payment
I wish to pay by Cred

☐ Visa ☐ Mastercard

Issuing Bank No.

Expiration Date

Signature X

Ship To The Fo
Name
Street

While it may be fun to look at wine labels, chocolate boxes, or candy bars in order to stimulate one's appetite for food or fonts (depending on your preference), most of us definitely do not enjoy an equally prevalent kind of communication: forms.

If you think about it, you'll have to admit that business forms process a lot of information that would be terribly boring to have to write afresh every time. All you do is check a box, sign your name, and you get what you ask for. Unless, of course, you're filling out

The "generic" look of most business forms usually derives from technical constraints. But even when those restrictions no longer exist, the look lingers on, often confirming our prejudice against this sort of standardized communication.

your tax return, when *they* get what they ask for; or unless the form is so poorly written, designed, or printed (or all of the above) that you have a hard time understanding it. Given the typographic choices available, there is no excuse for producing bad business forms, illegible invoices, awkward applications, ridiculous receipts, or bewildering ballots. Not a day goes by without one's having to cope with printed matter of this nature. It could so easily be a more pleasant experience.

While onscreen forms offer a very reduced palette of typographic choices, they at least provide some automatic features to help with the drudgery of repeatedly typing your credit card number.

These are some of the new typefaces designed to work well on low-resolution output devices, such as inkjet printers and the screen.

Typefaces designed with technical constraints.

Typefaces used for business communications have often been designed for a particular technology – optical character recognition, needle printers, monospaced typewriters, and other equipment.

What was once a technical constraint can today become a trend. The "nondesigned" look of OCR-B, the good old honest typewriter faces, even the needle printer, and other low-resolution alphabets have all been exploited by designers to evoke certain effects.

If you want to avoid any discussion about the typefaces you're using in your letters or invoices, you can fall back onto Courier, Letter Gothic, or other monospaced fonts (see page 125), even though they are less legible and take up more space than "proper" typefaces. You could be slightly more courageous and try one of those new designs that were created specifically to address legibility and space economy, as well as reader expectations.

.Handgloves

BASE 9

.Handgloves

LUCIDA

.Handgloves

ITC OFFICINA

.Handgloves

VERDANA

.Handgloves

LETTER GOTHIC

.Handgloves

COURIER

.Handgloves

OCR-B

Every PC user today knows what a font is, calls at least some of them by their first name (e.g., Helvetica, Verdana, and Times) and appreciates that typefaces convey different emotions. Although what we see on screen are actually little unconnected square dots that trick our eyes into recognizing pleasant shapes, we now expect all type to look like "print."

When each egg has data stamped on it, we wonder how the type got there. Does each chicken have its own little rubber stamp? Or do all the eggs roll by a machine, which gently impresses onto that most breakable of surfaces? And do different sorts of eggs have different types on them? Brush Script for free-range (see page 163), Copperplate for the expensive gourmet ones from geese and Helvetica for battery eggs?

While there is a tendency to overdesign everything and push technology to do things it was never intended to do, like printing onto raw eggs, at least we can continue our typographic training even when deciding whether the food we bought is nourishing or not.

We don't know whether the makers of Brunello di Montalcino deliberately chose the tall type for the labels on their wine bottles, but the widely spaced figures and the robust caps possess a certain elegance. As Monotype shows with their Andale Mono (which comes free with Microsoft software), there is room for good design even within the constraints of monospaced system fonts. Bar codes and OCR numbers are inseparable, but even that generic alphabet has already inspired a whole new type. And if you must imitate the printing on eggshells, FF Atlanta has the blotchy outlines needed to do so convincingly. While the makers of dot matrix printers try to emulate real logos, the designers of real fonts deliver the tools to print your supermarket receipts.

.HANDGLOVES

FF ATLANTA

.Handgloves

ANDALE MONO

.Handgloves123

FF OCR F LIGHT

.Handgloves123

FF OCR F REGULAR

.Handgloves123

FF OCR F BOLD

.Handgloves

FF DOT MATRIX TWO

E 5

4 | Frankfurt

555

Köln Mitte

Köln Süd

555

Bonn

Rodenkirchen

350 m

Köln   Köln   Köln

A Din-Schrift, reversed out.

B Type on back-lit sign suffers from radiant light.

C More explicit letter shapes help (*o* is more oval, dots are round).

Some of the most pervasive typographical messages have never really been designed, and neither have the typefaces they are set in. Some engineer, administrator, or accountant in some government department had to decide what the signs on our roads and freeways should look like. This person probably formed a committee made up of other engineers, administrators, and accountants who in turn went to a panel of experts that would have included manufacturers of signs, road safety experts, lobbyists from automobile associations, plus more engineers, administrators, and accountants.

Din (Deutsche Industrie-Norm= German Industrial Standard) is the magic word for anything that can be measured in Germany, including the official German typeface, appropriately (and not surprisingly) called Din-Schrift. Since it's been available in digital form, this face has been picked up by many graphic designers who like it for its lean, geometric lines, features that don't make it the best choice for complex signage projects.

You can bet there wasn't one typographer or graphic designer in the group, so the outcome shows no indication of any thought toward legibility, let alone communication or beauty. Nevertheless we're stuck with our road signs. They dominate our open spaces, forming a large part of a country's visual culture.

The letterforms on these signs were constructed from simple geometric patterns rather than from written or drawn letterforms because they had to be re-created by signmakers all over the country. It seems our official alphabets are here to stay, even though it would be possible to use other typefaces more suitable for the task.

Signage systems have to fulfill complex demands. Reversed type (e.g., white type on a blue background) looks heavier than positive type (e.g., black on yellow), and back-lit signs have a different quality than front-lit ones. Whether you have to read a sign on the move (from a car, for example), or while standing still on a well-lit platform, or in an emergency – all these situations require careful typographic treatment. In the past these issues have been largely neglected, partly because it would have been almost impossible to implement and partly because designers chose to ignore these problems, leaving them up to other people who simply weren't aware that special typefaces could help improve the situation.

Typefaces have now been designed with a series of closely related weights to offer precisely the right one, whether it's for a back-lit dark sign with white type, or for just black words on white, lit by the sun from above. The PostScript™ data generated with these types in drawing and layout applications can be used to cut letters of any size from vinyl, metal, wood, or any other material used for signs.

There are no more excuses for badly designed signs, whether on our roads or inside our buildings.

Inform

Black on white looks thinner than white out of black. Different weights can compensate for that effect.

D But still, backlighting presents a problem.

E The type has to be just a little lighter, so that finally ...

F ... It is more legible than in example B. This typeface is FF Info.

CHAPTER 2

What is type?

IMP CAE
TRAIAN
MAXIMO
ADDECIA
MONSETLC

13A

Ever since people have been writing things down, they have had to consider their audience before actually putting pen to paper: letters would have to look different depending on whether they were to be read by many other people (in official documents or inscriptions), just one other person (in a letter), or only the writer (in a notebook or a diary).

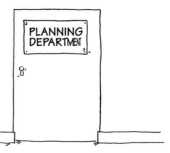

Graphic design and typography are complicated activities, but even simple projects benefit from thinking about the problem, forming a mental picture of the solution, and then carefully planning the steps between.

There would be less room for guesswork if letter shapes were made more formal as the diversity of the readership expanded.

The official Roman alphabet, as displayed in this detail of the Trajan Column in Rome, never went out of fashion.

Below: Many digital typefaces evoke the timeless beauty of ancient inscriptions and early printing types. Trajan, designed by Carol Twombly in 1990, is a good example.

Some of the first messages to be read by a large number of people were rendered not by pens but by chisels. Large inscriptions on monuments in ancient Rome were carefully planned, with letters drawn on the stone with a brush before they were chiseled. Even if white-out had existed in those days, it would not have helped to remove mistakes made in stone. A bit of planning was also more important then, since stonemasons were sometimes more expendable than slabs of marble or granite.

SENATVS·POPVLVSQVE·ROMANVS

IMP·CAESARI·DIVI·NERVAE·F·NERVAE

TRAIANO·PRETTY·LEGIBLE·DACICON

MAXIMO·TRIB·POT·XVIII·IMP·VI·COS·VI·P·P

ADDECLARANDVM·VERY·SPACED·OUT

arboscelli, & di floride Geniste, & di multiplice herbe uerdissime, quiui uidi il Cythiso, La Carice, la cómune Cerinthe. La muscariata Panachia ria el fiorito ramunculo, & ceruicello, ouero Elaphio, & la seratula, & di uarie assai nobile, & de molti altri proficui simplici, & ignote herbe & fiori per gli prati dispensate. Tutta questa læta regione de uiridura copiosamente adornata se offeriua. Poscia poco piu ultra del mediano suo io ritrouai uno sabuleto, ouero glareosa plagia, ma in alcuno loco dispersamente cum alcuni cespugli de herbatura. Quiui al gliochii mei uno iocundissimo Palmeto se appresento cum le foglie di cultrato mucrone ad tãta utilitate ad gli ægyptii. del suo dulcissimo fructo fœcunde & abundante. Tra lequale racemose palme, & picole alcune, & molte mediocre, & laltre drite erano & excelse, Electo Signo de uictoria per el resistere suo ad lorgente pondo. Ancora & in questo loco non trouai incola, ne altro animale alcuno. Ma peregrinando solitario tra le non densate, ma interuallate palme spectatissime, cogitando delle Rachelaide, Phaselide, & Libyade, non essere forsa a queste comparabile. Echo che uno affermato & carniuoro lupo alla parte dextera cum la bucca piena mi apparue.

In turn, these "official" styles of writing influenced how handwriting was looked at and how it was taught in schools or other learning centers, such as monasteries.

Today, when we are supposed to write legibly, we're instructed to "print." While we might have a hard time reading something written 200 years ago in what was then considered a very "good" hand, we have no problem reading writing from Roman times. Likewise, the typefaces designed 500 years ago, shortly after printing with movable type was invented, still look perfectly familiar (if a little quaint) to us. We might not be using the exact same letters reproduced in the identical manner, but the basic shapes and proportions are still valid today.

Page from Aldus Manutius' Hypnerotomachia Poliphili, 1499.

For centuries, *fraktur* (literally, "broken writing") was the standard typographic style in Northern Europe. Roman typefaces were called Roman because they came from Italy and were used to set Romance languages like Italian, French, and, of course, Latin.

When communications became more international, typefaces that were more universal were in demand. Today fraktur, gothic, and similar styles are only used to evoke the feeling of a bygone era, for example, on the banner of newspapers such as *The New York Times*.

They also come in handy when someone has to design a job that has Germanic undertones. The Nazis did indeed sponsor and even order (as was their way) the use of what they called "Germanic" typefaces, making it impossible for generations after World War II to use these types without unpleasant connotations.

Far left: Type designed by Francesco Griffo for Aldus Manutius' press. Bembo from the Monotype Corporation, 1929, is a modern equivalent.

Left: Gutenberg's Bible from 1455.

Some typefaces have stood the test of time and appear as contemporary today as they did 500 years ago. Their modern digitized versions have a slight edge when it comes to clean outlines.

Other typefaces also were perfectly legible 500 years ago, but can hardly be read by anybody today. It has to do with cultural perceptions, not the physical properties of the typefaces.

ſl ſi ſp ſl ſt ſſ ſh ſ ct v ff

Primieramente'imparerai di fare'que=
ſti dui tratti, cioe -'
da li quali ſe' principiano tutte'

Prıncipē de eodem officio. Cormicularium.
Comentarienſem. Numerarios. Adiutorem.
Abactis. A libellis. Exceptores & cęteros
officiales

oßervare' la sottoſcritta norma
&
Primieramente' imparerai di fare'
queſti dui tratti, cioe -
dali quali ſe principiano tutte'
le littere' Cancellareſche,
Deli quali dui tratti l'uno é piano et
groſſo, l'altro é acuto et sotti
le come' qui tu puoi vedere'
notato

While the basic shapes of our letters haven't changed much in hundreds of years, there have been thousands of variations on the theme. People have designed alphabets from human figures, architectural elements, flowers, trees, tools, and all sorts of everyday items, to be used as initials or typographic ornaments (see right).

Typefaces for reading, however, are generally derived from handwriting. Gutenberg's types followed the forms of the letters written by professional scribes in fifteenth-century Germany. The printers in Venice, a few decades later, also based their first types on local handwriting. Over the centuries, cultural differences have been manifested in the way people write. Professional scribes in European courts developed elaborate formal scripts. As literacy spread, people began to care more about expressing their thoughts quickly, and less about style and legibility.

Top inset: Italian manuscript, ca. 1530, shows how people wrote then. **Bottom inset:** From a book of writing instructions by Ludovico degli Arrighi, printed from engraved woodblocks, ca. 1521. The type on the page is Adobe Jenson Italic, designed by Robert Slimbach in 1996.

Quills, fountain pens, pencils, and felt-tip pens have all done their part to change the look of handwriting. The common denominator, the Roman alphabet, has survived all these developments remarkably intact.

H Gill Floriated Capitals, Eric Gill
A Mythos, Min Wang and Jim Wasco

N Tagliente Initials, Judith Sutcliffe
D Rad, John Ritter

A Bickham Script, Richard Lipton

G Rosewood, Kim Buker Chansler
L Giddyup, Laurie Szujewska

O Kigali Block, Arthur Baker
V Zebrawood, Kim Buker Chansler

E Studz, Michael Harvey
S Critter, Craig Frazier

By the same token, what was thought to be a fashionable house hundreds of years ago is still a very desirable house today. Fashion has changed considerably since the 1400s, but people still wear shirts, trousers, socks, and shoes. The process of manufacturing them has changed, but materials such as wool, silk, and leather are still very popular, and are often more desirable than their modern alternatives.

After all, the form of the human body hasn't changed in the last 500 years, nor has the basic way we look at the world around us. Our view of things is still largely shaped by nature – plants, animals, weather, scenery. Most of what we perceive as harmonious and pleasing to the eye follows rules of proportion that are derived from nature. Our classic typefaces also conform to those rules; if they don't, we regard them as strange: at the least fashionable, and at the worst illegible.

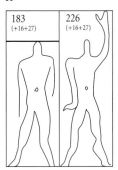

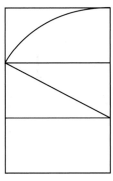

The human body hasn't changed drastically for centuries, so neither have things like shoes, fashion influences not-withstanding. Here is a collection of some footwear from the fifteenth century until today.

Some people have measured the human body to find what makes certain proportions look more beautiful than others.

Le Corbusier's Modulor (the system framing his ideas of modern functional architecture) is neatly related to a man with an outstretched arm. Not surprisingly (to anyone who's ever looked into the laws of harmonious proportions), the French architect found that the Golden Section was the underlying principle for all the measurements used in his drawings of the human body.

screen
copy

TECHNOLOGY RULES

TECHNOLOGY DESIGNS

TECHNOLOGY LEADS

The first generation to grow up with television (those born in the 1950s) is still imitating and fantasizing about the lifestyles depicted on TV. This generation is followed by one growing up with music videos, virtual reality, and the internet. The manipulation of sounds and images, the invention of artificial realities, and the experience of life inside man-made surroundings put to question our "natural" rules of perception. And, as with every technological and cultural development in the last 2000 years, type and typography reflect this. If current trends are anything to go by, the look of typefaces is bound to change more by the year 2020 than it has in all the years since the fifteenth century. The next generation of readers might consider things acceptable and, indeed, highly legible, that we would today consider ridiculous.

"It'll never catch on." Isn't that what people said about almost every major discovery or invention?

First examples of a new technology rarely resemble their modern counterparts, at least not in appearance. The underlying principles, however, were there already. If they hadn't been, planes wouldn't fly, TV tubes would implode, and cars wouldn't be faster than horse-drawn carriages.

Screen fonts for phones and handheld devices brought back bitmaps, just after we had got used to "real" printing type on our printers and computer screens. At the same time, font technology enables designers to re-create every style of lettering that ever existed, from nostalgic Americana to primitive pixel type, which is now being used as a fashion statement.

From top to bottom: Zuzana Licko's bitmap-inspired typefaces from 1987; screen fonts for Nokia, Ericsson, and Sony; Nugget and Jackpot by House Industries; FF Peecol and FF Sub Mono by Eboys.

Typefaces are **NOT intrinsically** legible

Send me a message

Ruf mich zurück.

Learning from Las Vegas
World Famous Buffet

Pixels are cool.
Pixels are way cool.

Sometimes a cigar is just a cigar.

Sigmund Freud (1856 –1939), known as the father of psycho-analysis, was an Austrian neurologist who developed techniques of free association of ideas and theorized that dreams are representative of repressed sexual desires. Things said without any forethought sometimes result in what is known as a "Freudian slip."

CHAPTER 3

Looking at type

HEAD

have to be big and at the top

Display *type is meant to show off the advantages* **of the product inside the package it is printed on.**

Type in books hasn't changed much over the last five hundred years. Then again, the process of reading hasn't changed that much either. We might have electric lights, reading glasses, and more comfortable chairs, but we still need a quiet corner, a little time on our hands, and a good story. Paperbacks crammed full of poorly spaced type with narrow page margins are a fairly new invention, born out of economic necessities, i.e., the need to make a profit. Chances are the more you pay for a book, the closer its typefaces resemble good historical models that date back to the Renaissance. By the time we are adults, we have read so much that is set in what are considered "classic" typefaces that we all think Caslon, Baskerville, and Garamond are the most legible typefaces ever designed …

Newspaper typography has created some of the very worst typefaces, typesetting, and page layouts known to mankind. Yet we put up with bad line breaks, huge word spaces, and ugly type because that is what we are used to. After all, who keeps a newspaper longer than it takes to read it? And if it looked any better, would we still trust it to be objective?

Small print is called small print even though it is actually only the type that is small. To overcome the physical limitations of letters being too small to be distinguishable, designers have gone to all sorts of extremes, making parts of letters larger and/or smaller, altering the space in and around them so ink doesn't blacken the insides of letters and obscure their shapes, or accentuating particular characteristics of individual letters. Another trick is to keep the letters fairly large, while at the same time making them narrower than is good for them or us so more of them will fit into the available space. Often enough, however, type is kept small deliberately so that we have a hard time reading it – for example, in insurance claims and legal contracts.

INES

Anyone looking at a printed message will be influenced, within a split second of making eye contact, by everything on the page: the arrangement of various elements as well as the individual look of each one. In other words, an overall impression is created in our minds before we even read the first word. It's similar to the way we respond to a person's presence before we know anything about him or her, and then later find it difficult to revise our first impression.

We read best what we read most, even if it is badly set, badly designed, and badly printed. This is not to suggest there is a substitute for good type, great design, or clean printing, but is merely a reminder that certain images are deeply ingrained in the reader's mind.

Graphic designers, typesetters, editors, printers, and other communicators are well advised to be aware of these expectations. Sometimes it may be best to follow the rules; at other times the rules need to be broken to get the point across. Good designers learn all the rules before they start breaking them.

.**Handgloves**
FUTURA EXTRA BOLD COND.

.**Handgloves**
ANTIQUE OLIVE BLACK

.**Handglo**
FF ZAPATA

.**Handgloves**
HOBO

.Handgloves
ADOBE CASLON REGULAR

.Handgloves
SWIFT LIGHT

.Handgloves
FF META BOOK

A recurring element on these pages, as first seen on page 19, is the "Handgloves." This word contains enough relevant shapes to judge an alphabet but is a change from the industry standard "Hamburgefons." The Handgloves show off typefaces used in the sample settings or referred to in the text.

Designing typefaces for particular purposes is more widespread than most people think. There is special type for telephone books, small ads, newspapers, and Bibles, and for the exclusive use of corporations. There are also typefaces designed specially to comply with technical constraints, i.e., low-resolution printers, screen displays, monospaced typewriters, and optical character recognition. So far, all these typefaces have tried to emulate historical models. Even bitmaps have become such a model, albeit one born of necessity. Below are types that have been designed for special purposes.

Bell Centennial
designed for telephone books.

ITC Weidemann
originally designed for a new edition of the Bible.

Spartan Classified
made especially for small ads in newspapers.

Corporate A
Daimler Chrysler's corporate typeface.

Sassoon Primary
for teaching handwriting to schoolchildren.

1

2

3

4

5

6

a	b
Cooper Black	MESQUITE

c	d
Arnold Böcklin	CAMPUS

e	f
Tekton	*Snell Roundhand*

This is a typographic puzzle. Which typeface do you think fits which shoe? The answers are on the next page, but don't look now – that would be cheating. Remember which letter from the boxes on this page goes with which number from the opposite page, then turn the page and check against our personal favorites.

In some cases it is very easy to spot a typographic faux pas.

1d CAMPUS

2b MESQUITE

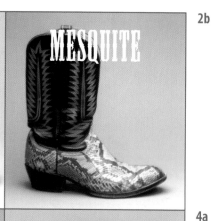

3f *Snell Roundhand*

4a **Cooper Black**

5b Arnold Böcklin

6e Tekton

No one would use the same shoes to go dancing, run a mile, climb the north face of the Eiger, and walk to the office – not many people, anyway. While your feet may pretty much stay the same shape, they need different types of support, protection or, indeed, enhancement to perform all the above tasks and many others besides.

This also applies to type. Sometimes the letters have to work hard to get across straight facts or numbers, or they may need to dress up the words a little to make them seem more pleasant, more comfortable, or simply prettier.

Some shoes fit your feet better than others, and you get to like them so much that you just want to keep buying the same kind over and over. Your friends, however, might begin to give you a rough time over your taste in footwear, so why not buy a few pairs of the same model but in different colors? Now you have more choices at the same comfort level.

Where's the analogy with type? Well, you can print it in different colors, on different backgrounds, dark on light or light on dark. It will always appear as if you are actually using more than one typeface.

Your personal choice of typefaces to match the shoes will probably be quite different from the ones shown here. With more fonts to choose from than there are shoes in your typical shoe store, the task is daunting.

Luckily, the intended typographic purpose narrows the choice down as much as where you will be wearing your shoes. Fortunately for the fashion-conscious designer, there are many options, even for similar design applications.

Cooper Black – see opposite page – is a very popular typeface, and was even more so thirty-five years ago. It has its advantages: nice and cuddly, heavy, and relatively unusual. But if you think it's been used a little too often, you can try Goudy Heavyface, ITC Souvenir Bold, Stempel Schneidler Black, or ITC Cheltenham Ultra. Compare them with each other and you will see they're all quite different, but might do the same job just as effectively.

Not all of us want to be seen wearing the same shoes as everybody else.

.**Handgloves**

GOUDY HEAVYFACE

.**Handgloves**

ITC SOUVENIR BOLD

.**Handgloves**

STEMPEL SCHNEIDLER BLACK

.**Handgloves**

ITC CHELTENHAM ULTRA

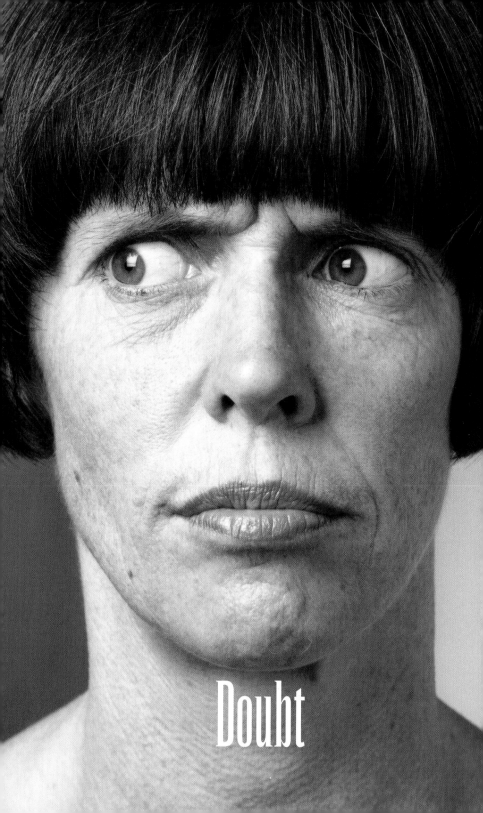

Doubt

So type has its practical uses – it can walk, run, skip, jump, climb, and dance. Can it also express emotions? Of course. If you look closely at a letter, you can see personality expressed in its physical characteristics: light or heavy, round or square, slim or squat. Letters can stand at attention next to each other like soldiers or they can dance gracefully on the line. Just as some words sound better than others, some words look nicer than others. That may be because we don't like the meaning of the word, but often we've formed an opinion before we've even read it. Isn't it nice that the *o* imitates the way we make our lips round to pronounce it? And how could the *i* stand for anything but the pointed sound it has in "pick"?

Dark emotions call for a black typeface with sharp edges; pleasant feelings are best evoked by informal, light characters. Or are they? The trouble is that as soon as you select a typeface that looks appropriate, put it on a page, surround it with space and perhaps other elements, it can take on a totally different look. So for the moment, we'll stick to choosing appropriate typefaces.

Runic Condensed is a typeface from Monotype. Released in 1935, it replicates a late nineteenth-century display type.

Bodega Sans adopts ideas from the high period of Art Deco. It was designed by Greg Thompson in 1990; its serifed companion followed in 1992.

Block is a family of typefaces originally designed by H. Hoffmann in 1908, with many subsequent versions released through 1926. Block simplified the setting of justified display lines with a system of capital and lowercase letters of varying widths that allowed the compositor to use the more extended alternate characters to fill out short lines. Block was the staple jobbing font for German printers well into the 1960s, when phototypesetting replaced hot metal. The irregular "mealy" outlines appeal to a modern audience, who like that recycled, used-before look.

Neville Brody designed the movie titles for *A Rage in Harlem*. In 1996, he was persuaded to turn that design into a full family of typefaces. The informal weight is aptly named Harlem Slang.

In 1937 Morris Fuller Benton designed Empire for *Vogue* magazine. David Berlow revived it in 1989, adding an italic and a lowercase, both unavailable in the original.

Runic Condensed is slightly awkward and definitely not suited for long passages. Its spiky serifs and exaggerated letterforms do not agree with classic ideals of beauty and fine proportion. If unusual letterforms express uneasy feelings, these other condensed types might be a good choice.

Doubt?
Runic Condensed

Doubt?
Bodega Sans Light

Doubt?
Bodega Serif Light

Doubt?
Block Extra Condensed

Doubt?
Harlem Slang

Doubt?
Bureau Empire

Surprise

Some words are much more fun to find an appropriate typographic equivalent for than others. (Surprise, surprise.) It may be fairly difficult to find a majority agreement on the right typeface to spell "doubt," but this one shouldn't cause any problems.

What's more unexpected, more surprising, than someone's handwriting? The best casual typefaces have always managed to carry some of the spontaneity of handwritten letters into the mechanical restrictions of typesetting. Even the names of some typefaces make you want to choose them. How about this one: Mistral – a cool wind blowing from the north into southern France. And indeed, in the south of France it seems to have become the standard typeface for every shopfront and delivery van.

In case you don't agree that Mistral suggests surprise, here are some alternatives.

Mistral was designed by Roger Excoffon in 1955. His other typefaces – Antique Olive, Choc, Banco – also show a characteristic Gallic style and have been enormously successful in France and other European countries.

Susanna Dulkinys' Letter Gothic Slang replaced some characters with others that have similar shapes, but different meaning. The *S* is a dollar sign; the *p* is the thorn – used in Icelandic, Old English, and phonetics; the *i* is an upside-down exclamation mark used in Spanish for quotes; and the *e* is a currency sign.

The complete freedom offered by computer applications makes type even more flexible – if a word doesn't look right when first set, you can manipulate the outlines until it does exactly what you want.

"Surprise" is shown at right in its unaltered form. We didn't like the join between *S* and *u*, so we created outlines in Adobe Illustrator, cleaned up that detail (and a few others), and placed it in our photograph, where you can see the revised word. Most people would believe that it had been written by someone with a felt-tip pen, not simply set as part of a complete page.

Mistral

Letter Gothic Slang

Dogma Script

Dizzy

Ottomat Bold

JOY

The more characters in a word, the more chances there are to find the right letterforms to express its meaning. This word doesn't give us many choices, just three characters: *j o y* or *J O Y*. Seeing that the lowercase *j* and *y* look so similar, an all-capital setting will work better with this one. All three typefaces here have a generous feel to them – open forms with confident strokes and a sense of movement.

ITC Kabel, Syntax, and Lithos are modern interpretations of classical letterforms; they maintain a chiseled look without formal stroke endings, which are known as *serifs*.

The letter *Y*, a latecomer to the Latin alphabet, is called *i grec* in French (Greek *i*). Its shape is derived from one of the calligraphic variations of the Greek upsilon.

The original Kabel, designed by Rudolf Koch in 1927, has distinct Art Deco overtones, whereas International Typeface Corporation's 1976 version has a very generous x-height and is more regular and less quirky.

JOY
ITC Kabel Book

Syntax has the proportions of ancient Roman letters, but no serifs, making it both contemporary and classic looking. It was designed by Hans-Eduard Meier in 1968. A completely redesigned and expanded version was released by Linotype in 2001.

JOY
Syntax

Lithos is Carol Twombly's 1989 rendering of Greek inscriptions – just as elegant as Roman capitals, but less restrained. This face became an instant success (graphic designers still use it for all sorts of trendy purposes), which goes to show that a classic can also be cheerful and modern.

JOY
Lithos Regular

.Handgloves
ITC KABEL BOOK

.Handgloves
SYNTAX

.HANDGLOV
LITHOS REGULAR

It is nice to see words typeset so their own explanations are carried in the letters. These free and easy shapes certainly make you think of a joyful person with arms in the air.

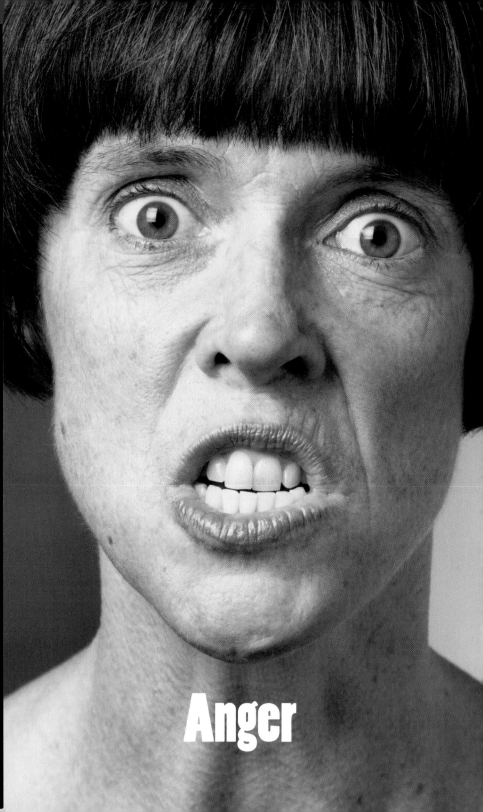

Anger

Anger, like doubt, can be described as a dark feeling that calls for a black, heavy typeface. Anger is not as narrow as doubt. It needs room to expand, sometimes to shout out loud.

It helps if the letters are not perfectly worked out and closed in on themselves, but rather a little irregular, leaving room for our imagination. A well-balanced Univers or Helvetica would not do.

Most really black typefaces have been overused because there aren't enough choices for the designers of posters and tabloid newspapers. These kinds of faces can be set with hardly any space between letters, which makes a large impact in a small space.

Futura Extra Bold and ITC Franklin Gothic Heavy have been favorites for a long time. Inspiration for Solex – designed by Zuzana Licko in 2000 – reportedly came from two principal sources: Alternate Gothic and Bauer Topic (also known as Steile Futura) and is her exploration of the industrial sans serif genre. Eagle is FontBureau's 1989 adaptation of Morris Fuller Benton's famous titling, Eagle Bold, drawn – caps only – in 1933 for the National Recovery Administration. Officina Black adds weight to the 1990 sans and serif family; the new versions were digitized by Ole Schäfer. Giza brings back the glory of the Victorian era. David Berlow based the family (1994) on showings in Figgins' specimen of 1845.

And all the way from the 1960s, Roger Excoffon's Antique Olive Nord shows that good typefaces are indestructible.

Flyer Extra Black Condensed, designed in 1962 by Konrad Bauer and Walter Baum.

Anger!
Flyer Extra Black Condensed

Poplar is a 1990 revival from Adobe of an old wood type from the mid-nineteenth century.

Anger!
Poplar

Block Heavy (1908) is the fattest member of the family. Its outlines are deliberately irregular, which helped prevent damage when metal type was printed on heavy platen presses. You could call it a pre-stressed design.

Anger!
Block Heavy

Anger!
Angst Heavy

Angst and Franklinstein are both rightly named. Jürgen Huber and Fabian Rottke designed them – respectively – in 1997 for FontFont's Dirty Faces™ group.

Anger!
Franklinstein

. Handgloves
FLYER EXTRA BLACK CONDENSED

. Handgloves
FUTURA EXTRA BOLD

. Handgloves
POPLAR

. Handgloves
ITC FRANKLIN GOTHIC HEAVY

. Handgloves
SOLEX BLACK

. Handgloves
GIZA NINE THREE

. Handgloves
ITC OFFICINA BLACK

. Handgloves
EAGLE BLACK

. Handgloves
BLOCK HEAVY

. Handglo
ANTIQUE OLIVE NORD

Handgloves

MvB Sirenne

Handgloves

Thesis Sans 5

Handgloves

Freestyle Script

HANDGLOVES

Ironwood

Carta

There are seven deadly sins, seven seas, and seventh sons of seventh sons, but thousands of typefaces. Someone had to come up with a system to classify them, since describing how different type designs express different emotions just isn't exact enough. Unfortunately, there is not only one system, but quite a few, all of them too involved for anyone but the most devoted typomaniac. So here's the most rudimentary method of classifying type. It's not historically correct, nor does it give a complete overview of the available choice of fonts. It simply shows that with just a few basic principles, hundreds of ways of designing typefaces become possible, the same way a few basic emotions evoke a million ways to make a face.

The unofficial type classification – do not confuse with the official one on this page.

In case anyone wants it for the record: here's the official Adobe type classification. We have chosen a typical typeface for each category, trying to avoid all the best-known ones.

VENETIAN

Handgloves
Centaur

GARALDE

Handgloves
Sabon

TRANSITIONAL

Handgloves
Janson Text

DIDONE

Handgloves
ITC Bodoni

SLAB SERIF

Handgloves
Memphis

SANS SERIF

Handgloves
Syntax

GLYPHIC

Handgloves
Friz Quadrata

SCRIPT

Handgloves
Ex Ponto

DISPLAY

HANDGLOVE
Charlemagne

BLACKLETTER

Handgloves
Wilhelm Klingspor Gotisch

SYMBOLS

Universal News and Commercial Pi

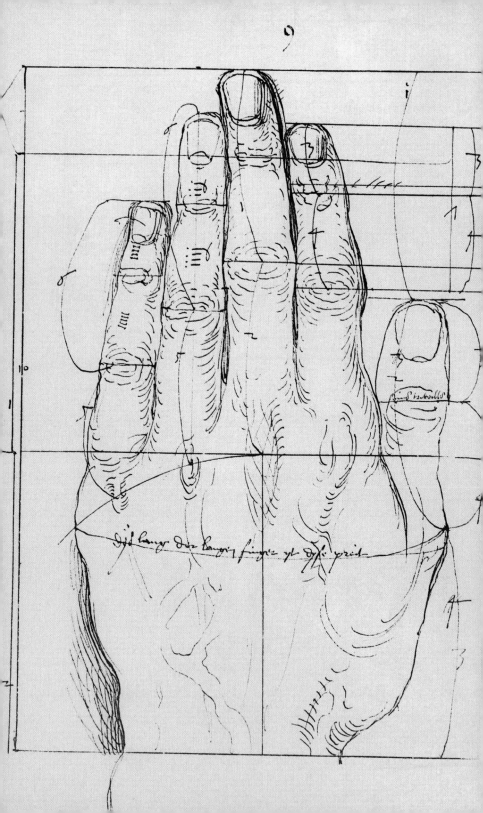

Scientists have not been content with just calling the human face "beautiful" if it meets certain ideals, or "ugly" if it doesn't. They had to go out and measure proportions of nose to jaw, forehead to chin, and so on, to establish why some faces are more appealing than others.

Typographers and graphic designers often choose typefaces for the very same reason they might fancy a person: they just like that person. For more scientifically minded people, however, there are specific measurements, components, details, and proportions to describe various parts of a letter. While these won't tell you what makes a typeface good, they will at least give you the right words to use when you discuss the benefits of a particular face over another. You can say "I hate the x-height on Such-a-Gothic" or "These descenders just don't work for me" or "Please, may I see something with a smaller cap height?" and you'll know what you are talking about.

Albrecht Dürer tried to figure out what makes the human body look beautiful by measuring the proportions of the parts.

By now you will have noticed that we use the words *typeface* and *type* to describe what people these days refer to as a *font*. Much of the terminology used today comes from the era of metal type. The spaces between lines are still (and not very accurately) described as *leading*, even though they certainly aren't made up of strips of lead anymore. A font was a prescribed grouping of letters from one typeface assembled by a typefoundry for sale. These were apportioned to the number of letters used most frequently in any given language. The English printer who bought a French font of type, for instance, soon noticed its lack of sufficient k and w and its large supply of q. Italian demands a larger number of c and z; Spanish, far more of d, t, and all the vowels; German, more capital letters and more z, but less y.

We design typefaces and we produce fonts. And throughout this book, we maintain that distinction. While the language of typography still adheres to some rules, there really aren't any standards for type designers to follow. Typographic features, such as large x-heights, wide counters, and exaggerated ascenders, are no less slaves to fashion than the perpetual changes in skirt lengths determined on Paris runways. The size of type, indicated in points (a point is .01384 inch; 12 points = 1 pica; 6 picas = 1 inch), is only a reminder of a historical convention, when type was cast on a body of metal. The body size of all 12-point type would have been the same, but the actual image on that body could be vastly different. Have a look at the 20-point types below – they don't have very much in common apart from the baseline.

The moral?
What you see is what you get – trust your eyes, not the scientific measurements.

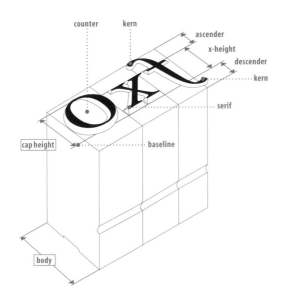

Sizes Sizes Sizes Sizes Sizes

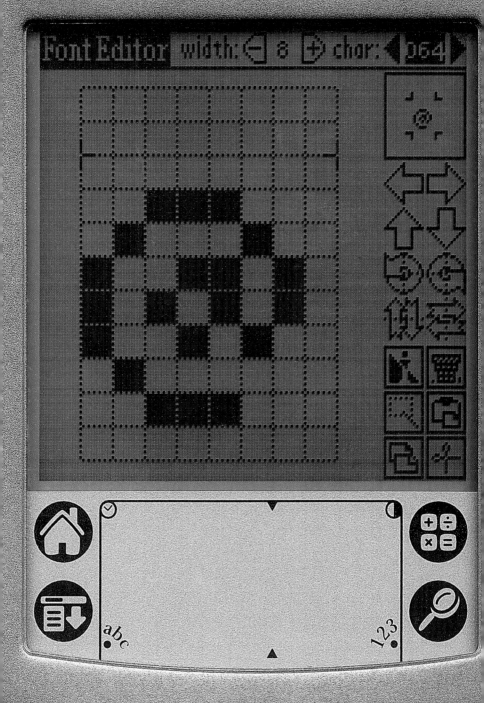

While metal letters could be made to any width and height, digital type has to conform to multiples of the smallest unit: the pixel. Every character has to be a certain number of pixels wide and high. This is not a problem when the letters are made up of 600 pixels per inch (or about 24 pixels per mm), as is the case with modern laser printers – those pixels are not discernible to our eyes, and we are happy to believe that we are looking at smooth curves instead of little squares fitted into tight grids.

A font editor on a palmtop device is the perfect tool to pass the time on an airplane or in a waiting room. Click away for a few hours, and by the time you land in Rio or get in to see your acupuncturist you have your own exclusive font. It may not be as legible as the pre-installed one, but no-one else will have the same font!

On screens, however, only 72 pixels make up one inch (roughly three pixels per mm). We could see each and every one of them if engineers hadn't already found ways around that (read more on page 121). Computer screens, however, are not where we read all of our type these days – phones, PDAS, even microwave ovens all have displays. Most screen displays are small and simple, which means black on greenish gray. And the type unmistakably consists of bitmaps: this means that an 8-point letter is actually made up of eight pixels. If we allow six pixels above the baseline (see previous page spread), including accents, and two below for descenders, that leaves only three or four pixels for a lowercase character. Despite these restrictions, there are hundreds of bitmap fonts, each unique by a matter of a few pixels, but enough to prove that typographic variety cannot be suppressed by technological restraints.

Editing pixels is like a game of chess: there are only a few black and white squares, and every move has enormous consequences.

Rather than try and imitate Times New Roman or Helvetica on a tiny chessboard, bitmap fonts have to make virtue out of necessity. It is amazing to see how much one can push the critical shape of each letter toward some almost abstract black and white graphic, and still make us think we're reading roman characters.

Joe Gillespie has designed a series of very small bitmap fonts for use on screens, appropriately named Mini 7, which is the size they are supposed to be set in. Another set of bitmap fonts for tiny sizes (only three pixels tall!) comes from Eboys, who have turned the bitmap look into an art form.

The makers of devices with small display screens would be well advised to look at these examples and in the future keep their engineers from making bitmap fonts.

HANDGLOVES
HANDGLOVES
HANDGLOVES
HANDGLOVES
HANDGLOVES
Handgloves
Handgloves

The Mini series, all at 7pt. In the first five lines, capital letters are five pixels tall, while the mixed words have that many pixels for a lowercase letter.

Handgloves
Handgloves

FF Xcreen only uses three pixels for a lowercase character, but as this is not a true bitmap but actually an outline font, the pixels can be scaled to any size, and range from the sublime to the ridiculous.

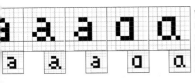

What a difference a dot makes: with only five pixels for the x-height, a designer of bitmap types has to be content moving one pixel at a time.

The best part about playing
the piano is that you don't have
to lug around a saxophone.

Gerry Mulligan (1927–1996),
master of the baritone saxophone, was one of the most
versatile figures of modern
jazz. He wrote his first arrangements and jazz compositions
when he was still in his teens,
and was part of the cool jazz
scene in the 1940s; especially
noteworthy were his pianoless
groups in which his intricate
and carefully balanced com-
posing and arranging brought
improvisation to new heights.
He occasionally played the piano.

CHAPTER 4

Type with a purpose

You know what it's like. It's late at night, your plane leaves at 6 AM, you're still packing, and you just can't decide what to put into that suitcase.

Picking typefaces for a design job is a very similar experience. There are certain typefaces you are familiar with. You know how they will behave under certain circumstances, and you know where they are. On the other hand, there are those fashionable types that you've always wanted to use, but you're not quite sure if this job is the right one to experiment on. This is just like choosing which shoes to take on your trip – the comfortable ones are not the height of fashion, but the fashionable ones hurt. You might be able to stand them for a short reception, but not for shopping, let alone for a hike into the countryside.

Before you pack your font suitcase, you need to look at the task ahead. Strike a balance between practicality and aesthetics – that's what design is all about.

While nobody has ever classified typefaces according to their problem-solving capabilities, many typefaces we use today were originally designed for particular purposes. Some of them are mentioned on page 39, but there are many more. Times New Roman was specially produced in 1931 for the London newspaper that gave its name to the typeface.

In the late 1930s, Mergenthaler Linotype in the USA (led by Chauncey H. Griffith) developed a group of five typefaces designed to be legible despite the rigors of newspaper printing. They were, not surprisingly, called the "Legibility Group," and two of them are still very popular today: Corona and Excelsior.

It might seem odd that legibility has to be a special concern when designing a typeface, but there are plenty of types around that are meant to be seen, not read; these typefaces are very much like clothes that look great but barely protect the wearer from the elements.

Gulliver is Gerard Unger's solution for many problems in newspaper design and production. It fits 20% more copy into the columns without sacrificing legibility and is sturdy enough to be carelessly printed on recycled paper. *USA Today* uses it, among other newspapers around the world.

Coranto is Unger's latest typeface for newspapers. Designed in 1999, it is being used for *The Scotsman* as well as newspapers in Sweden and Brazil.

Tobias Frere-Jones' work on Poynter was sponsored by the Poynter Institute to answer the same question: how to retain copy without losing readers? As we read best what we read most, the designer stuck to familiar forms and returned to Hendrik van den Keere's seventeenth-century oldstyle roman. As different methods of reproduction and printing may add or reduce weight by a fraction, Poynter Oldstyle Text is offered in four grades.

.Handgloves

TIMES NEW ROMAN

.Handgloves

CORONA

.Handgloves

EXCELSIOR

.Handgloves

GULLIVER

.Handgloves

CORANTO

.**Handgloves**

POYNTER OLDSTYLE BOLD

hand   hand   hand   hand

PoynterText One   PoynterText Two   PoynterText Three   PoynterText Four

Going on vacation doesn't necessarily mean traveling to a warm climate, but it always means we can leave behind many of our conventions, including the way we normally dress – or have to dress, as the case may be. You pick your clothes according to what is practical: easy to pack, easy to clean, and according to what is fun: casual, colorful, loose, and maybe a little more daring than what you would wear in your hometown.

The typographic equivalents are those typefaces that are comfortable to read, but which may be a little more idiosyncratic than your run-of-the-mill stuff. Serifs, too, can be casual, and "loose fit" is actually a typesetting term describing letters that have a comfortable amount of space between them.

As it happens, quite a few of the very early typefaces from the Renaissance and their modern equivalents fit that description. They still show their kinship with Italian handwriting, which by necessity had to be more casual than rigid metal letters. If you were a scribe in the papal office and had to write hundreds of pages every day, you wouldn't be able to take the time to fuss over formal capitals. So the scribes developed a fluent, cursive handwriting, which today we call italic, because it was invented in Italy.

You will have noticed that this whole page is set in a script font, and it feels quite comfortable. A conventional rule says that you can't set whole pages, let alone books, in the italics of a typeface. The only reason it might not work is because we're not used to it. As pointed out on page 39, we read best what we read most. But that's no reason not to take a vacation from our daily habits and look at something different, at least once a year.

Some typefaces have a leisurely look about them while conforming to everyday typographic expectations. Others were born with unusual, yet casual, shapes and make the best of it.

Stempel Schneidler combines friendly letter shapes with high legibility – you can use it every day without it becoming restrictive like a necktie.

A recent typeface that looks casual, even "nice," but is still good for real work is ITC Flora. It was designed by the Dutch type designer Gerard Unger in 1980 and named after his daughter. Ellington, released in 1990, is a design by Michael Harvey, the English lettering artist and stone carver. Both typefaces are quite unusual and therefore not often thought of as useful text faces. But they are.

Many typefaces designed to look "friendly" tend to appear patronizing. They can be so nice that you quickly get tired of them. When you're looking for casual typefaces, the obvious candidates are, of course, scripts. Most, however, are not suited to long spells of reading, just as sandals are very comfortable, but not when walking on rocky roads.

To make a typeface look as casually elegant as FF Fontesque takes a lot of experience and effort. Nick Shinn designed Fontesque in 1994. It wasn't his first design, and it shows.

Cafeteria indeed started on Tobias Frere-Jones' napkin, and he managed to balance activity with legibility in this freeform sans serif face.

.Handgloves

STEMPEL SCHNEIDLER

.Handgloves

ITC FLORA

.Handgloves

ELLINGTON

.Handgloves

FF FONTESQUE

.Handgloves

CAFETERIA

Most type is used for business communication of one sort or another, so it has to conform to written and unwritten rules of the corporate world. Just as business people are expected to wear a suit (plus, naturally, a shirt and tie), text set for business has to look fairly serious and go about its purpose in an inconspicuous, well-organized way. Typefaces, such as Times New Roman and Helvetica, fit this bill perfectly, not by their particular suitability but more by their lack of individualism.

However, just as it is now permissible in traditional business circles to wear fashionable ties and to even venture into the realm of Italian suits that are not black or dark blue, typographic tastes in those circles has widened to include other type-faces, from Palatino to Frutiger.

Generally, it is very simple to classify a particular business by the typefaces it prefers: the more technical a profession, the cooler and more rigid its type-faces (Univers for architects); the more traditional a trade, the more classical its typefaces (Bodoni for bankers).

The trouble is, there is no law against speculators employing a true classic, trust-worthy typeface in their brochures, lending these unsavory entities typographic credibility, although nothing else.

To show the subtle differences between fonts at this size, we've set the copy at left in a variety of types, one for each paragraph. Handgloves at the bottom of this column show them in sequence.

Frutiger, originally designed in 1976 by Adrian Frutiger for the signage at the Charles de Gaulle airport in Paris, has become one of the most popular typefaces for corporate use.

Palatino, designed by Hermann Zapf in 1952, owes its popularity – especially in the USA – largely to its availability as a core font on PostScript laser printers. It is nevertheless a welcome alter-native to other, less suitable, serif fonts.

Adrian Frutiger designed Univers in 1957. It was the first typeface to be planned with a coordinated range of weights and widths, comprising twenty-one related designs, recently expanded to 59 weights (see page 85).

ITC Bodoni is one of many re-designs of Giambattista Bodoni's classic typefaces from the late eighteenth century. It shows more color and stroke variations than other Bodoni revivals, and is available in three versions for different sizes.

.Handgloves

FRUTIGER

.Handgloves

PALATINO

.Handgloves

UNIVERS

.Handgloves

ITC BODONI SIX

.Handgloves

ITC BODONI TWELVE

.Handgloves

ITC BODONI SEVENTY-TWO

2

If it were just a little heavier, News Gothic by Morris Fuller Benton, 1908, would be a favorite workhorse typeface. ITC Franklin Gothic, a 1980s redesign of Benton's original typeface from 1904, has more weights as well as a condensed and a compressed version plus small caps.

Lucas de Groot designed his Thesis family from the outset with 144 weights. The Thesis Sans family has become an alternative to Frutiger in corporate circles, as it is both neutral and versatile. Lucida Sans, by Kris Holmes and Charles Bigelow, 1985, has sturdy, rugged letter shapes. Its sister typeface, Lucida, remains one of the best choices for business communications printed on laser printers and fax machines.

FF Meta has been called the "Helvetica of the 1990s." While that may be dubious praise, Meta is a warm, humanist alternative to the classic sans faces. Lots of detail make it legible in small sizes and "cool" rather than neutral. You should also consider the condensed weights of Frutiger as useful, but underused alternatives.

Designed by Martin Wenzel in 1999, FF Profile is one of a new generation of modern sans faces.

The real winner has to be this very face, Myriad, designed by Carol Twombly and Robert Slimbach in 1991. Myriad is neutral enough to stay in the background, but has that little extra personality to shine when necessary.

■ Calling a typeface "a real workhorse" doesn't mean that others don't work, it just means that it is one of those that doesn't look very glamorous and is consequently not likely to be known by name; such types, however, are used every day by designers and typesetters because of their reliability.

● If you set a catalog for machine parts, or instructions for using a fire extinguisher, you're not worried about subtly curved serifs or classical contrast. You need letters that are: clearly distinguishable; compact, so enough of them fit into a limited space (is there ever enough space?); and sufficiently sturdy to withstand the rigors of printing and copying.

Here's what is needed in a hardworking typeface:

1 A good regular weight – not so light that it will disappear on a photocopy (everything, it seems, gets copied at least once these days), and not so heavy that the letter shapes fill in.

2 At least one bold weight, with enough contrast to be noticed, to complement the regular weight.

3 Very legible numerals – these must be particularly robust because confusing figures can be, in the worst of cases, downright dangerous.

4 Economy – it should be narrow enough to fit large amounts of copy into the available space, but not actually compressed beyond recognition. A typeface fitting this description would also fare very well when faxed.

ITC Officina Bold

Handgloves
Handgloves
News Gothic

Handgloves
Handgloves
Franklin Gothic

Handgloves
Handgloves
Thesis Sans

Handgloves
Handgloves
Lucida Sans

Handgloves
Handgloves
Lucida

Handgloves
Handgloves
FF Meta

Handgloves
Handgloves
FF Meta Condensed

Handgloves
Handgloves
Frutiger Condensed

Handgloves
Handgloves
ITC Officina

Handgloves
Handgloves
FF Profile

Handgloves
Handgloves
Myriad

One
of the few sanctuaries for old
aristocratic traditions is
Society. **Snell Roundhand**

*Top hats, cummerbunds, patent
leather shoes, and coats with tails are all
remnants of the eighteenth century,
when countries were run by
kings and queens who spoke French to
each other and their entourages.*

NOT **FF Scala Jewels**
*much of that remains, except for maîtres
d'hôtel at posh restaurants who fake French
accents and wear coats with tails.*
Künstler Script

OF COURSE, **Mrs. Eaves**
*French is still the official language
of the diplomatic corps.
Typographically speaking, we have reminders of these
somewhat antiquated traditions in the accepted and
expected ways of designing invitations and programs.*
Mrs. Eaves Italic

CENTERED TYPE AND
A PREFERENCE FOR FONTS THAT COME
FROM A GOOD BACKGROUND IN
COPPER ENGRAVING OR
UPPER-CRUST CALLIGRAPHY.
Copperplate

And, of course,
Matrix Script Inline
those very familiar four letters, »rsvp«, which mean
»please let us know whether you're going to be there,«
but actually stand for »Répondez s'il vous plaît.«
Suburban Light

There is no category known as "formal fonts," but a number of typefaces come from that background. The text at left is set in Snell Roundhand, a formal script from the 1700s, redesigned in 1965 by Matthew Carter.

Apart from formal scripts such as Snell, Künstler Script, and others like it, there are the aptly named copperplates. They look formal and distinguished and are even available in a range of weights and versions, but they all lack one important feature: lowercase characters.

Other typefaces that owe their appearance to the process of engraving into steel as opposed to writing with a quill or cutting into wood are Walbaum, Bauer Bodoni, or ITC Fenice. They can look formal and aristocratic enough to make a favorable impression when printed on fine paper.

While FF Scala Jewels is an extension of the FF Scala family (a contemporary interpretation of classic book typefaces) by Martin Majoor from 1993, Mrs. Eaves is Zuzana Licko's 1996 idiosyncratic take on Baskerville. It is named after Sarah Eaves, the woman who became John Baskerville's wife. Licko's Matrix Script Inline from 1992 gets closer to American vernacular, and Rudy VanderLans' 1993 Suburban connects classic scripts with, well, suburban neon signs. And, as VanderLans proudly proclaims, Suburban is the only typeface in existence today that uses an upside-down *l* as a *y*.

Base 9 Small Caps

FF Letter Gothic

Going out on the town allows us to do the things we don't get to do in the office, and permits us to wear all the trendy stuff that we can never resist buying but don't really need on a day-to-day basis.

What makes typefaces trendy is unpredictable – much to the chagrin of the people who have to market them. A corporation, a magazine, a TV channel can pick a typeface, expose it to the public, and a new typographic fashion can be born. But, as with fashion and pop music, it usually takes more than one designer in the right place at the right time picking the right font off a web site or out of a catalog.

Trendy types

Modula Outline

There are typefaces that are only suitable for the **more** occasional occasion. **They might be** too hip **to be used for mainstream communication, or they could simply be too uncomfortable – a bit like** wearing very tight jeans rather than admitting that they don't fit us any longer. Very often these offbeat fonts are both – **tight in the crotch** and extroverted.

FF Din

FF Din Condensed

Typography is as much a mirror of what goes in society as the styling of mobile telephones or car radiators. Cars still take half a dozen years from concept to production, so their designers have to anticipate trends. Since cars are icons of our mobile society, their designs, in turn, create trends.

funfonts

Interstate Bold Condensed

Interstate Light

The entertainment value of this sort of typographical work is often higher than that of the straightforward corporate stuff, so there's a great deal of satisfaction gained not only from the words, but also from the fun of being able to work with really unusual fonts .

Fashionable faces

OCR-A

One thing leather jackets have on trendy typefaces is that the jackets get better as they get older, which is more than can be said about some of the typefaces we loved in the 1970s but would be too embarrassed to ask for now. Like all fashions, however, they keep coming back. Don't throw away your old fonts – keep them for your kids.

FF Typestar Normal

While technology allows us to produce a font in weeks – if not hours – from rough sketches or ideas, it still takes a few years for a typeface to get to market and to the attention of the typeface-buying public. Right now, early in the twenty-first century, we are seeing a return to the time-honored classics and their modern interpretations. We have also learned to live with bitmaps, both as a necessity and as a fashion statement. Most industrial type styles have been exploited, from monospaced typewriter faces through electronic font generators to industrial signage. And some of the most-used typefaces were first produced for the signs above our freeways. Interstate is Tobias Frere-Jones' interpretation of the white-on-green letters in the USA, while FF Din expands the model used on Germany's autobahn. Ironically, typefaces designed for one particular purpose often seem to look really good on just about anything else.

NOAH'S NEW YORK BAGEL
THE MARINA

NOAH'S

NEW YORK
THE MARINA

As long as you print on paper, the choice of typeface is governed first and foremost by the content of the message, then the intended audience, and only lastly by technical constraints. When we move from almost limitless resolution on paper to shapes generated by cathode rays or liquid crystal, we enter a world of optical illusions. To make up for the lack of high fidelity our eyes have to be tricked into seeing lifelike images rather than spots of colored light (see page 121). On the screen, colors are not created from CMYK: cyan, yellow, magenta, and black (the k stands for "key"), but are broken down into RGB: red, green, and blue; letters are composed of coarse lines or dots, and black is not an ink, but the absence of light.

Typefaces have to work very hard under these conditions – there is no room here for leisure fonts, nor for scripts, nor some of the trendy faces that hide more than they reveal. The workhorses for "old" media still work well in the new. Rugged construction, clear counter spaces, easily discernible numerals, and well-defined weights have all been mentioned before as prerequisites for anything that has to be read under less than ideal circumstances. And no matter what progress technology brings in the future – human eyes will never be comfortable staring into light coming from a screen.

Architectural type has to compromise between materials and legibility. A mosaic made up of millions of pieces would allow for smoother lettershapes, but would be neither as durable nor as affordable as one with coarser bits. Using only triangular elements comes fairly close to what our eyes perceive as round shapes.

Matthew Carter's Verdana has become a very successful face on paper as well, while Bigelow & Holmes' Lucida, initially designed for laser printers in 1983, looks great in high-resolution, and is one of the best screen fonts around. FF Typestar by Steffen Sauerteig has rugged shapes reminiscent of typewriter faces is suitable for extreme conditions on screen or paper.

All those minute details that make a good typeface pleasant to behold and easy to read, actually add noise on a screen. However, the absence of these details would make the type look cold and technical, as if generated by machines and legible to them alone.

The designer of typefaces suitable for onscreen reading has to balance the requirements of a precise but cold medium (light emitted by all manner of tubes, crystals, diodes, and plasms) against our need for subtle contrast and soft shapes. And as most of what we read on screen eventually gets printed as well, alphabets have to offer enough traditional beauty to be acceptable against the familiar competition of the past 500 years.

Slightly extended letter shapes have more open counters and are thus more legible, but need more space around them. Subtle contrast between thin horizontals and thicker verticals doesn't translate well into single pixels, and the tiny serifs that look delicate in display sizes will only add noise at 10pt or less on screens.

The screen fonts offered by Microsoft and Apple work well under all circumstances, but have become too ubiquitous to lend an individual note. Adobe Web Type features twelve Adobe Originals optimized for easy onscreen viewing. The typefaces have been fine-tuned to provide maximum legibility. The package even includes script and decorative fonts.

And if a text is mainly meant for the screen and for very small sizes, pure bitmap fonts work well. If you print them, the pixels are small enough to all but disappear. This is 7pt Tenacity Condensed, a bitmap font from Joe Gillespie.

Handgloves
Look at these faces at very small sizes & you get an idea of how well they will perform on screen

Handgloves
Look at these faces at very small sizes & you get an idea of how well they will perform on screen

Handgloves
Look at these faces at very small sizes & you get an idea of how well they will perform on screen

No, Watson, this was not done by accident, but by design.

Sherlock Holmes is a fictional detective created by Sir Arthur Conan Doyle (1859–1930). Holmes' extraordinary powers of deductive reasoning carry him, along with his somewhat befuddled partner Dr. Watson, through some of the most complex mysteries in detective fiction.

CHAPTER 5

Type builds character

The Way to Wealth

BENJAMIN FRANKLIN

If time is of all things the most precious, wasting time must be the greatest prodigality; since lost time is never found again, and what we all time enough always proves too little. Let us then be up and doing, and doing to a purpose, so by diligence we should do more with less perplexity. Sloth makes all things difficult, but industry all things easy. He that riseth late must trot all day and shall scarce overtake the business at night; while laziness travels so slowly that poverty soon overtakes him. Sloth, like rust, consumes faster than labor wears, while the used key is always bright. Do not squander time, for that's the stuff life is made of; how much more than is necessary do we spend in sleep, forgetting that the sleeping fox catches no poultry, and that there will be sleeping enough in the grave.

So what signifies wishing and hoping for better times? We may make these times better if we bestir ourselves. Industry need not wish, and he that lives upon hope will die fasting. There are no gains without pains and he that has a trade has an estate, and he that has a calling has an office of profit and honor. But then the trade must be worked at and the calling well followed. Though you have found no treasure, nor has any rich relation left you a legacy, diligence is the mother of good luck, and all things are given to industry. Plow deep while sluggards sleep, and you will have corn to sell and keep; work while it is called today or you know not how much you may be hindered tomorrow: one today is worth two tomorrows, and farther: have you something to do tomorrow, do it today.

Be ashamed to catch yourself idle. When you have so much to do, be up by the peep of day. Let not the sun look down and say: "Inglorious here he lays." Handle your tools without mittens; remember, that the cat in gloves catches no mice. It is true there is much to be done, and perhaps you are weak-handed, but stick to it steadily, and you will see great

The way books are read hasn't changed very much over the last 500 years, so the way books look hasn't had to change either. Only the economics have changed, which means that publishers today insist on fitting more type onto a page, and they aren't always prepared to pay for good typesetting, let alone for someone to actually design the inside of a book, and not just its cover. Every additional dollar spent on the manufacture of a book adds seven or more dollars to its retail price.

The lefthand pages in this chapter have been reduced to fit into this book; most are about two-thirds their optimum size.

Cheap paperbacks, therefore, do not usually represent the state of the typographic art. In general they could be nicer than they are because it costs no more to observe the basic rules of book layout using a good, legible typeface than to ignore these rules and set the text in whatever the printer happens to have around.

To show just how much type can accomplish and how versatile it is, we have used the same text, written by Benjamin Franklin in 1733, to set all the samples in this chapter; some liberties have been taken with Mr. Franklin's words to make typographic points.

Our example here is set in Adobe Caslon, Carol Twombly's 1990 version of one of the most popular of all the book faces (originally designed by William Caslon in 1725); we also use the Adobe Caslon Expert set (see page 107). The Irish playwright George Bernard Shaw insisted that all his books be set in Caslon, earning him the title "Caslon man at any rate." For decades the motto of British printers was, "When in doubt, set it in Caslon."

The layout follows the classic model with wide margins, generous space between lines, and a centered title. To achieve a nice, smooth edge on both sides of the column, the punctuation is hung in the righthand margin.

.Handgloves

ADOBE CASLON

. HANDGLOVES

ADOBE CASLON EXPERT

. 🦌🐚🦋🐚🦋🦌

ADOBE CASLON ORNAMENTS

Frugality will never go out of style.

To be secure, certainty and success rely on a dependable financial institution.

It's easy to think that a little tea or a little punch now and then, a diet a little more costly, clothes a little finer, and a little entertainment is no great matter. But at the Bank of Benjamin we think that being aware of small expenses is just as important as the consideration it takes, say, to purchase a home: small leaks will surely sink a great ship. Our financial advisors will always be available to advise the best ways to put your savings to work. We know that what often appears to be a terrific investment quite frequently turns out otherwise. So when confronted by a great pennysworth, our advisors will pause a while: Cheapness is apparent only, and not real. We want our customers to enjoy their hard-earned leisure without having to think about their hard-earned dollars. So be sure to keep this in mind: if you won't listen to reason, it will rap your knuckles.

The Bank of Benjamin

Our advisors are at your service 24 hours a day. Please call us:

1-800-SAVINGS

There also seems to be a generic style for advertisements. Although display advertising does not have a lengthy tradition (it has only been around about 150 years), its style is as established as that of the traditional book.

Headline on top, attention-grabbing picture underneath, subhead, main copy, logo, pay-off line, address, URL, or telephone number. Never more than eight elements! People are able to comprehend at most about that many different components in one message; as soon as there are more, comprehension requires too much effort, and attention goes elsewhere.

You can also recognize a serious, idea-based advertisement by the serious typography. No experiments here – take a classic, well-tried typeface, arrange it in a predictable layout, and people may actually read your message.

When Paul Renner started work on Futura in 1924, it was proclaimed as the "typeface for our time," alluding to the social democratic reform of German society in the 1920s. The first weight was released in 1927.

What is more no-nonsense than Futura, the typeface made respectable in those first VW ads from the 1950s and 1960s? They were truly revolutionary, using this cool, restrained German typeface to promote that strange little car.

Futura is still one of the most popular typeface families, providing art directors all over the world with some of the best bold, extra bold, and condensed fonts available. Advertising certainly wouldn't be the same without Futura.

.Handgloves
FUTURA BOOK

.Handgloves
FUTURA BOOK OBLIQUE

.Handgloves
FUTURA CONDENSED BOLD

.Handgloves
FUTURA CONDENSED BOLD OBLIQUE

.Handgloves
FUTURA HEAVY

.Handgloves
FUTURA HEAVY OBLIQUE

.Handgloves
FUTURA BOLD

.Handgloves
FUTURA BOLD OBLIQUE

.Handgloves
FUTURA EXTRA BOLD

.Handgloves
FUTURA CONDENSED EXTRA BOLD

.Handgloves
FUTURA COND. EXTRA BOLD OBLIQUE

.Handgloves
FUTURA EXTRA BOLD OBLIQUE

.Handgloves
FUTURA LIGHT

.Handgloves
FUTURA LIGHT OBLIQUE

.Handgloves
FUTURA CONDENSED LIGHT

.Handgloves
FUTURA CONDENSED LIGHT OBLIQUE

.Handgloves
FUTURA

.Handgloves
FUTURA CONDENSED

.Handgloves
FUTURA CONDENSED OBLIQUE

.Handgloves
FUTURA OBLIQUE

Time Line

A lecture
by Frank Franklin

If time is the most precious of all things, wasting time must be the greatest sin. Lost time is never found again, and what we call enough time is never enough. Let us then be up and doing, and doing with a purpose, so by diligence we should do more with less perplexity. Sloth makes all things difficult, but industry all things easy. He that riseth late must trot all day and shall scarce overtake the business at night; while laziness travels so slowly that poverty soon overtakes him. Do not squander time, for that's the stuff life is made of; how much more than is necessary do we spend in sleep, forgetting that the sleeping fox catches no poultry, and that there will be sleeping enough in the grave.

Saturday, December

7:00 p.m.

PacBell Park

You may think, perhaps, that a little tea, or a little punch now and then, diet a little more costly, clothes a little finer, and a little entertainment now and then, can be no great matter. Watch those little expenses, a small leak will sink a great ship, and moreover, fools make feasts, and wise men eat them. Buy what you have no need for and before long you shall sell your necessities. Many a one, for the sake of finery on the back have gone with a hungry belly. Silks and satins, scarlet and velvets, put out the kitchen fire. By these and other extravagances the genteel are reduced to poverty.

He that riseth late must

trot all day and

shall scarce overtake the

business at night

Remember this, however, if you won't be counseled, you can't be helped, and further: If you will not listen to reason, it will surely rap your knuckles.

If you won't | be counseled | you can't be helped

The computer has given us access to a design language that would have been far too complicated without the aid of sophisticated programs and a page description language such as PostScript. Gradations of color, overlaid images, frames, lines, boxes, background, foreground – all add up to the appearance of the page as one image, rather than a linear sequence of elements.

This particular layout at the left can be classified as "New Wave, circa 1987." The availability of millions of images and thousands of fonts (not to mention 16.7 millions of colors) at the click of a mouse seem to make every perceivable style and fashion – past and future – easy to emulate, if not invent.

Luckily for professional designers, this sounds easier than it is. If everybody could be a successful designer by following simple recipes, we'd be out of work tomorrow. But that extra ingredient, a concept, an idea, cannot be formulated as readily as this. The waves may come and go, but graphic design will always be about problem solving first, and style-making afterward.

For this exercise, we have not shown everything we could on a page. We haven't gone crazy with sampling images, overlaying them as if there were no tomorrow, or using the weirdest fonts available.

Instead, we've picked the typeface that has pretty much replaced Helvetica as Corporate World Font Number One. Frutiger (see page 65) is now available in a good range of weights and widths, making it suitable for almost every typographic task. It avoids Helvetica's blandness, adding instead a humanist touch. This improves legibility by keeping letter shapes open and more distinct from one another.

The condensed weights are particularly suitable for projects that need a clean-looking, highly legible, relatively neutral, and space-saving typeface.

.Handgloves
FRUTIGER 45 LIGHT

.Handgloves
FRUTIGER 55 ROMAN

.Handgloves
FRUTIGER 65 BOLD

.Handgloves
FRUTIGER 75 BLACK

.Handgloves
FRUTIGER 95 ULTRABLACK

.Handgloves
FRUTIGER 57 ROMAN CONDENSED

.Handgloves
FRUTIGER 67 BOLD CONDENSED

.Handgloves
FRUTIGER 77 BLACK CONDENSED

.Handgloves
FRUTIGER 87 EXTRABLACK COND.

Comparison of critical letter shapes in Akzidenz Grotesk, the mother of most modern sans serifs; Helvetica, the face without features; Univers, the cool alternative; Frutiger, the friendly sans; and Thesis, the typeface with 144 cousins in one family

aces

aces

aces

aces

aces

Industry need not wish; if you live on hope you will die fasting. If you have a trade, you have an estate, and if you have a calling you have an office of profit and honor.

*I*f time is the most precious of all things, wasting time must be the greatest sin; since lost time is never found again, and what we call enough time always proves to be too little. Let's be up and doing, and with a purpose, so by diligence we can do more with less perplexity.

Sloth makes all things difficult, but industry all things easy. If you get up late you must trot all day and barely may overtake the business at night; while laziness travels so slowly that poverty will soon overtake you. Sloth, like rust, consumes faster than labor wears, while the used key is always bright. Time is the stuff life is made of; how much more than is necessary do we spend in sleep, forgetting that the sleeping fox catches no poultry, and that there will be sleeping enough in the grave.

Industry need not wish, if you live on hope you will die fasting. If you have a trade, you have an estate, and if you have a calling you have an office of profit and honor. But then the trade must be worked at and the calling well followed.

F.F. Franklin
Chief Executive Officer

Though you have found no treasure, nor has any rich relation left you a legacy, diligence is the mother of good luck, and all things are given to industry. Plow deep while sluggards sleep, and you will have corn to sell and keep; work while it is called today or you know not how much you may be hindered tomorrow: one today is worth two tomorrows, and furthermore: if you have something to do tomorrow, do it today. If you want a faithful servant, and one that you like, serve yourself. Be circumspect and caring, even in the smallest matters, because sometimes a little neglect breeds great mischief: for want of a nail the shoe was lost, for want of a shoe the horse was lost, being soon overtaken and stolen by the enemy.

Pension Assets Exceed $12 Billion

So much for industry, and attention to one's own business, but to these we must add frugality, if we would make our industry more successful. We think of saving as well as of getting. You may think, perhaps, that a little tea, or a little punch now and then, a diet that's a little more

1

Corporations spend a good deal of money to show their shareholders, their customers, and their banks how good they are (the corporations, not the others). So they hire designers or advertising agencies (there is a difference) to design brochures, booklets, and annual reports to make them look as excellent as they wish they were.

Strangely enough, as anyone who's ever been on a design jury judging annual reports or other corporate messages can attest, many of these printed pieces come out looking very similar. Although some designers set trends and others follow them, they all get paid to make their clients look different from the competition.

It is, therefore, easy enough to design a typically corporate page, at least for the USA. In Europe, this page would look quite different, but with definite similarities within certain countries. You can always tell a German report from a Dutch, British, or Italian one, but they all have one thing in common: the picture of the chairman.

Judging from the typeface used, the page on the left must be for a financial or similar institution. It is set in Bodoni, and the layout combines classic elements, such as the centered sidebar, with traditional advertising conventions and justified text across a column that is far too narrow to achieve reasonable word breaks and word spaces (more about that in chapter 7).

While you can't go wrong with Bodoni, you could, however, try a different version now and again. Berthold, Linotype, and Monotype Bodonis are very much alike, whereas Bauer Bodoni has so much contrast between thick and thin lines that it isn't really suitable for small sizes. ITC Bodoni is much better at small sizes than all the others. Its little quirks become visible only at large sizes, which might be desirable, as they will add a little life to your pages.

The Bodonis have grown into a large family – everybody who is anybody in the type world offers a different version. Here are a few of the styles and weights available.

.Handgloves
BERTHOLD BODONI LIGHT

.Handgloves
BODONI BOOK

.Handgloves
BERTHOLD BODONI REGULAR

.Handgloves
ITC BODONI SEVENTY TWO

.Handgloves
BAUER BODONI BOLD

.Handgloves
BODONI

.Handgloves
BERTHOLD BODONI MEDIUM

.Handgloves
ITC BODONI BOLD SIX

.Handgloves
BAUER BODONI BOLD

.Handgloves
BODONI BOLD

.Handgloves
ITC BODONI BOLD TWELVE

.Handgloves
BAUER BODONI BLACK

.Handgloves
BAUER BODONI BLACK CONDENSED

.Handgloves
BODONI POSTER COMPRESSED

Order Form   Time Saving Books Ltd.

▷ *Time as a Tool.* **Benny Frank. Philadelphia: Caslon Publishing, 2002.**
790pp. Hardcover. $29.95.
From *Time as a Tool*: "If time is the most precious of all things, wasting time must be the greatest sin; since lost time is never found again, and what we call time enough always proves too little. Do not squander time, for that's the stuff life is made of; how much more than is necessary do we spend in sleep, forgetting that the sleeping fox catches no poultry, and that there will be sleeping enough in the grave."

▷ *Circumspection at Work.* **Fran Benjamin. Philadelphia: Caslon Publishing, 2002.**
145pp. Softcover. $12.95.
From *Circumspection at Work*: "So what signifies wishing and hoping for better times? We could make these times better if we bestir ourselves. Industry need not wish, and he that lives upon hope will die fasting. There are no gains without pains. If you have a trade you have an estate, and if you have a calling you have an office of profit and honor. But then the trade must be worked at and the calling well followed. Though you have found no treasure, nor has any rich relation left you no legacy, diligence is the mother of good luck, and all things are given to industry. Plow deep while sluggards sleep, and you will have corn to sell and keep; work while it is called today or you know not how much you may hindered tomorrow: one today is worth two tomorrows, and farther: have you something to do tomorrow, do it today."

▷ *Time & Saving.* **Jamie Franklin. Philadelphia: Caslon Publishing, 2003.**
220pp. Softcover. $12.95.
From *Time & Saving*: "We must consider frugality, if we want to make our work more certainly successful. A person may, if she doesn't know how to save as she gets, keep her nose all her life to the grindstone, and die not worth a penny at the last. A fat kitchen does make a lean will. Think of saving as well as of getting. A small leak will sink a great ship. Cheapness is apparent only, and not real; the bargain, by straitening you in business, might do you more harm than good. 'At a great pennyworth, pause awhile.' "

Sales Tax

We are required to collect sales tax on shipments to the states listed below. Please add the correct percentage amount. If you pay by credit card and don't know your sales tax, leave the line blank and we will fill in the correct amount.

_____ California
_____ Connecticut
_____ Florida
_____ Georgia
_____ Illinois
_____ Maryland
_____ Massachusetts
_____ Minnesota
_____ Missouri
_____ New Jersey
_____ New Mexico
_____ New York
_____ Ohio
_____ Pennsylvania
_____ Texas
_____ Virginia
_____ Washington

Ordering Information

Name

Address

City   **State**   **Zip**   **Country**

Telephone   **Date of Purchase**

Book Title   **Quantity**

Book Title   **Quantity**

Book Title   **Quantity**

Subtotal

Sales Tax

Shipping (please add $2 per book)

Total Order

Method of Payment

_____ Check or money order enclosed, payable to TimeSaving Books Ltd.

_____ Please charge my credit card

Credit Card Number   **Expiration Date**

_____ Visa/MasterCard   _____ American Express

Signature (required for credit card purchases)

One of the areas typographers usually stay well clear of is the design of forms. They are not the easiest things to design, and in that respect should be considered a challenge. They offer enormous rewards – not winning awards or being included in the design annuals, but in terms of achievement.

Forms always have too much copy, so first choose a font that is narrower than your run-of-the-mill ones. Make sure it is clearly legible, has a good bold weight for emphasis, and has readable numerals.

Keep the preprinted information clearly separated from the areas you want people to fill in. These lines should be inviting guides for people's handwriting, and not look like bars on a prison cell window. The same can be said of boxes around text. Who needs them? Some designers seem to be afraid that the type might fall off the page if there isn't a box around it: it won't happen! Without restricting boxes, forms don't look half as forbidding and official. Different areas on the page can be separated by white space, as shown in our example.

If any typeface was designed to be neutral, clean, and practical, it is Univers, designed by Adrian Frutiger, 1957. The condensed versions of this typeface are actually quite legible, considering how much copy can fit into a confined space.

Forty years later, Linotype started work on a new version of Frutiger's original design. The family now includes 59 weights plus four monospaced typewriter weights. While the old system featured a numerical system to distinguish the weights, with Univers 55 being the normal roman weight, the new Linotype Univers needs three digits. Basic regular is now 430. The first digit stands for weight, i.e., 1 is ultralight, 2 thin, etc., and 9 is extra black. The second digit denotes width, i.e., 1 for compressed, 2 for condensed, 3 for basic, and 4 for extended. The third indicates upright roman (0) or italic (1). Not exactly intuitive, but effective once you get used to it. Frutiger, Neue Helvetica, Centennial, and a few other Linotype faces are still classified according to the old system using two digits to signify weight and width or slant.

This table shows how all the weights of Univers relate to each other.

The numbering system makes sense – once you've thought about it.

110	120	121	130	131	140	141
210	220	221	230	231	240	241
310	320	321	330	331	340	341
410	420	421	430	431	440	441
510	520	521	530	531	540	541
	620	621	630	631	640	641
	720	721	730	731	740	741
	820	821	830	831	840	841
	920	921	930	931	940	941

BY FRANK BENJAMIN

The Time Is
NOW!

If time be of all things the most precious, wasting time must be the greatest prodigality; since lost time is never found again, and what we call time enough always proves little enough. Let us then be up and doing, and doing to a purpose, so by diligence we should do more with less perplexity. Sloth makes all things difficult, but industry all things easy. He that riseth late must trot all day and

shall scarce overtake the business at night, while soon overtakes him. Sloth, like rust, consumes faster than labor wears, while the used key is always bright. Do not squander time, for that's the stuff life is made of; how much more than is necessary do we spend in sleep, forgetting that the sleeping fox catches no poultry, and that there will be sleeping enough in the grave.

So what signifies wishing and hoping for better times? We may make these times better if we stir ourselves. Industry need not wish, and he that lives upon hope will die fasting. There are no gains without pains. If you have a trade you have an estate, and if you have a calling you have an office of profit and honor. But then the trade must be worked at and the calling well followed. Though you have found no treasure, nor has any rich relation left you a legacy, diligence is the mother of good luck, and all things are given to industry.

> **"Wise men learn by others' harms, fools scarcely by their own."**

Plow deep while sluggards sleep, and you will have corn to sell and keep; work while it is called today or you know not how much you may be hindered tomorrow: one today is worth two tomorrows, and farther: have you something to do tomorrow, do it today. If you want a faithful servant, and one that you like, serve yourself.

Be circumspect and caring, even in the smallest matters, because sometimes a little neglect breeds great mischief: for want of a nail the shoe was lost, for want of a shoe the horse was lost, being soon overtaken and stolen by the enemy, all for want of care of a horseshoe nail. You may think, perhaps, that a little tea, or a little punch now and then, diet a little more costly, clothes a little finer, and little entertainment now and then, can be no great matter: Many a little makes a mickle; beware of little expenses, a small leak will sink a great ship, and again, who dainties love shall beg-

Magazines are perhaps one of the best indicators of a country's current typographical taste; most of them get redesigned often enough to be on top of contemporary cultural inclinations. Magazine publishing is a very competitive business, and design plays a significant role in the way magazines present themselves to the general public.

Depending on the readership, magazines can look old-fashioned, conservative, pseudo-classic, trendy, cool, technical, newsy, and noisy. All these signals are conveyed by typography, which may or may not be an adequate representation of the editorial contents.

The textface above is FF Quadraat by Fred Smeijers. Its almost upright italic and overall condensed letterforms give away its Dutch origin. It is unusual enough to convey a diverence, but not so silly and overdesigned to distract from normal reading.

For our example, we have chosen to combine a very traditional layout with a not-so-traditional typeface. The page employs a lot of the paraphernalia of "good" editorial layout: drop capitals, letterspaced headers, scotch rules, large pull-quotes, italic lead-ins, and a contrasting bold sans serif to complement the serif text face.

The italic lead-in uses a bit of a gimmick with those diminishing sizes to attract attention and is just trendy enough to appeal to a readership of people between thirtysome-thing and the midlife crisis. These people are reportedly willing to read more than a couple of paragraphs in one sitting.

On close inspection at larger sizes, FF Quadraat looks as strange as the double *a* in its name. Since it was intended to be set in between 7 and 12 point for long copy and continuous reading, those seemingly exaggerated traits add up to character. No slick mechanical precision here, which may look cold to our eyes, but little quirks to delight the tired eye. Smeijers made thorough studies of hand punchcutting techniques and cut punches himself before he used the computer to digitize his drawings. In fact, he has written a book on the subject, called *Counterpunch*.

Franklin Gothic was also cut in steel punches back in 1904 when Morris Fuller Benton first designed the face for ATF. It, too, has kept a liveliness that is often missing from digital fonts. The little eccentricities helped to make Franklin Gothic the proverbial Anglo-Saxon sans serif. Even today, there are not many other typefaces that combine impact and friendliness as well.

.Handgloves
FF Quadraat Regular

.Handgloves
FF Quadraat Bold

.Handgloves
FF Quadraat Sans

.Handgloves
FF Quadraat Sans Condensed

.Handgloves
FF Quadraat Display

.Handgloves
Franklin Gothic Condensed

.Handgloves
Franklin Gothic Extra Cond.

.Handgloves
Franklin Gothic Demi

Good Times, Better Times

Francis Franklin

Be ashamed to catch yourself idle. When you have so much to do, be up by the peep of day. Handle your tools without mittens; remember, that the cat in gloves catches no mice. There is much to be done, and perhaps you are weak-handed, but stick to it, and you will see great effects, for constant dropping wears away stones; and by diligence and patience, the mouse ate in two the cable; and allow me to add, little strokes fell great oaks. If you want a faithful servant, and one that you like, serve yourself.

Be circumspect and caring, even in the smallest matters, because sometimes a little neglect breeds great mischief. For want of a nail the shoe was lost, for want of a shoe the horse was lost, being soon overtaken and stolen by the enemy, all for want of a horseshoe nail. So much for industry, and attention to one's own business, but we must add frugality to these if we want to make our industry more successful. A person may, if she doesn't know how to save as she gets,

New!

Wishing and hoping for better times? We can make these times better if we bestir ourselves. Industry need not wish, and if you live upon hope you will die fasting. If you have a trade, you have an estate, and if you are lucky enough to have a calling, you have an office of profit and honor. But the trade must be worked at and the calling well followed. Though you have found no treasure, nor has any rich relation left you a legacy, remember that diligence is the mother of good luck, and all things are given to industry. Work while it is called today because you don't know how much you may hindered tomorrow:

Today's lifestyle has one thing going for it: it provides tomorrow's nostalgia; as soon as things are far enough down memory lane, we invariably start looking at them with enchanted eyes.

The other good thing about nostalgia is that you can recycle ideas without being accused of petty larceny; people might even admire your interest in things historical. Frederic Goudy once said "The old guys stole all our best ideas" – we could certainly do worse than look to the past for typographic inspiration. After all, most of the typeface styles we now see have been around for a few hundred years, or at least several decades.

Old advertisements are always a source of amusement, and today we have access to digital versions of the typefaces our predecessors used. We can re-create early ads almost faithfully. A note of caution: if you imitate that old look too well, people might not realize that you're actually trying to tell (or sell) them something new.

The fonts used in our nostalgic ad all go back to the days of hot metal typesetting, when one typeface would have to serve the printer not only for setting advertisements, but also for things like invitations and stationery. Type was neither cheap nor as easily available as it is today, so a printer's investment had to go a long way. Letterpress printing meant that letters literally got pressed, and that pressure would leave its mark: the finer the type, the more it would show wear and tear. Jobbing fonts, as they were called, had to be strong enough to withstand the mechanical pressure and loud enough to be noticed. And being somewhat condensed to save precious space was certainly a bonus.

Every foundry had their own version of these hardworking typefaces. Hermes from Schriftguss AG was first produced around 1908, as was its twin, Berthold's Block. In the USA, William Hamilton Page patented his wood type in 1887. They all show a similar approach to the problem: blunt corners, low contrast, and soft outlines. If a letter already looked a little worn, one wouldn't notice the effects of bad treatment as obviously as one would with a sharp-edged Bodoni, for example.

Rhode is David Berlow's successful attempt to combine early English Grotesques – as made by Figgins at the beginning of the nineteenth century – and American advertising type, like the straight-sided Railroad Gothic, into a complete and large family of sans serifs. Quiet it is not, but it has great presence.

.Handgloves

RHODE BLACK CONDENSED

.Handgloves

RHODE BOLD CONDENSED

Matthew Butterick rendered four weights of his version of Hermes in 1995. It has the smudges of rough presswork built into the design itself. Hamilton was adapted by Tom Rickner in 1993. He followed the original bold weight and used it as the basis for his medium and light versions. While Hamilton Bold is already quite condensed, the Medium and the Light certainly don't waste any space with open counters or too-tall ascenders.

.Handgloves Handgloves **Handgloves**

HAMILTON LIGHT, MEDIUM, BOLD

.Handgloves

BERLINER GROTESK MEDIUM

.Handgloves

BLOCK REGULAR

.HANDGLOVES

FF GOLDEN GATE GOTHIC

.met and de of for het und

FF CATCHWORDS

.HANDGLOVES

FF PULLMAN INLINE

.Hand Hand **Hand Handgloves**

HERMES THIN, REGULAR, BOLD, BLACK

THE

DAILY INTEREST

Largest Circulation Anywhere

Boy Raised by $ea Otters Declared Financial Wizard

NATIONAL

EXCLUSIVE

ELVIS SEEN AT BANK

Be ashamed to catch yourself idle. When you have so much to do, be up by the peep of day. Don't let the sun look down and say: "Inglorious here she lays." Handle those tools without mittens; remember, that the cat in gloves catches no mice. It is so true there is much to be done, and perhaps you are weak-handed, but stick to it steadily, and you will see great effects, for constant dropping wears away stones; and by diligence and patience, the mouse ate in two the cable, and little strokes fell great oaks. If you want a faithful servant, and one that you like, serve yourself. Be circumspect and caring, even in the smallest matters, because sometimes a little neglect breeds great mischief: for want of a nail the shoe was lost, for want of a shoe the horse was lost, being soon overtaken and stolen by the enemy, all for want of care of a horse-shoe nail. *continued on pg. 12*

Aliens Open $1 Million Account in Tucson

Woman Faints While Waiting for Travelers Cheques
"I thought it was my new diet."

Think of saving as well as getting. A person may, if she doesn't know how to save it as she gets it, keep her nose all her life to the grindstone, and die not worth a penny. A fat kitchen does makes a lean will. You may think, perhaps, that a little tea, or a little punch now and then, a diet that's a little more costly, clothes a little finer, and little entertainment now and then, can be no great matter: Many a little makes a mickle; beware of those little expenses – a small leak will sink a great ship, and be reminded again that those who love dainties shall beggars prove, and moreover, fools make feasts, and wise men eat them. Buy what you don't need and before long you will sell your necessities. "At a great pennyworth, pause awhile." Cheapness is apparent only, and not real; the bargain, by straitening you in business, might

continued on pg. 12

Every society needs a diversion that doesn't do any physical harm, but keeps those people who prefer to live in fantasy worlds occupied. Certain newspapers cater to this segment of the populace, and the typographic styles reflect their journalistic attitude toward the truth.

How do you design stories about children born with three heads, or families that glow in the dark, or nine-month-old babies who can bench-press their moms? Easy: take bold, preferably condensed typefaces, randomly distort the shapes electronically, put outlines around them, mix several together, and insert on the same page.

We haven't quite dared to apply the same techniques in this book. Neither have we exposed our readers to the sort of illustrations these sensationalist newspapers use, although image-manipulation has never been so easy with such realistic results: it's almost too simple to depict a UFO hovering over West Virginia.

Once you start looking for really bold condensed fonts, you realize that there can never be enough of these, as every magazine needs headlines that shout and scream.

We mentioned the ever-present Futuras, Franklin Gothics, and Antique Olives on page 51, where we also showed Flyer, Block, and Poplar, as well as some newer alternatives. Most of these, however, are far too well behaved and good looking to use in a sensationalist way.

. Handgloves
AACHEN BOLD

. Handgloves
FF SARI EXTRA BOLD

. Handgloves
FORMATA BOLD CONDENSED

. Handgloves
INTERSTATE ULTRA BLACK COND.

. Handgloves
GRIFFITH GOTHIC ULTRA CONDENSED

. Handgloves
FF FAGO CONDENSED

. Handgloves
IMPACT

. Handgloves
TEMPO HEAVY CONDENSED

Design is Problem Solving

Designing for the web confronts us with a lot of limitations and challenges. It also offers new choices. As this is a book about type and typography, we cannot go into animations or sound, although both are possible and often desirable on a web page. We also can't go into the details of HTML or any other programing language. There are plenty of books available and, of course, a lot of information can be found online.

Design is problem solving

Solving problems and working with constraints is what separates real communication design from making pretty pictures – in any media. Three main constraints define web design: size/format, color, and type.

Landscape or portrait?

Most printed pieces – books, magazines, brochures, newspapers – are in portrait format, ie they are taller than wide. As computer monitors are wider than tall web pages also have to be in landscape format. And since monitors on desktops cannot be scaled to any size and are viewed from arm's length, a web page can't be as big as a poster.

Too wide to read

A landscape page across 600 pixels with 10 point type will yield lines with more than 120 characters, or 20 words. Half that amount would be ideal. If you make a narrower column to avoid the reader having to turn her head, you gain space at the side, ideally suited to accomodate those headlines and other emphasis you would have put in the middle of the text on a portrait format.

Leading is good

Adding more space between lines (aka leading) works wonders, too. Just try a few extra points of leading and legibility will be improved tremendously (see page 141).

Color is cheap

Color is an expensive luxury on paper, but comes free on the screen. Use it for emphasis or simply to make a page more attractive. Reverse type reads better on screen than it does on paper, but you should still use it sparingly.

Type is stupid

Italic type is simply stupid. The pixel grid is square and does not allow for old typographic traditions. You can't make type light either as you cannot have less than one pixel for a stroke. Go bold, go bigger, go color or create space for emphasis in text.

Traditional doesn't work

Times New Roman was designed for printing a newspaper. Helvetica for advertising. If you can't or won't use software which embedds your own fonts into the web page, at least use Cascading Style Sheets with fonts made for the screen. Verdana and Georgia were designed for this medium.

design is problem-solving.

As this is a book about type and typography, we cannot go into all the new choices designers have for web design, such as images, sound, or animation. There are plenty of books available and, of course, endless information can be found online.

Solving problems and working within constraints is what separates real communication design from making pretty pictures — in any media. A few obvious constraints define web design: size, format, color, type, and file size — but we'll ignore the last one here.

landscape or portrait?

Most printed pieces — books, magazines, brochures, newspapers — are in portrait format, i.e., they are taller than wide. As computer monitors are wider than tall, web pages also have to be in landscape format.

long lines are bad.

A landscape page across 600 pixels with 10-point type will yield lines with more than 120 characters, or 20 words. Half that amount is ideal, allows you to make narrower columns, and to put subheads next to the text.

leading is good.

Adding more space between lines works wonders, too. Just try a few extra points of leading and legibility will improve. (see page 141).

color is cheap.

Color is an expensive luxury on paper, but comes free on the screen. Reversed type reads better on screen than it does on paper, but you should use it sparingly — a page like this is almost too much.

type is simple.

Italic type ona screen is *simply stupid*. The pixel grid is square and does not allow for old typographic traditions. You can't make type light either, as you cannot have less than one pixel for a stroke. **Go bold, go bigger,** go color.

traditional is not safe any longer.

Times New Roman was designed for printing a newspaper, Helvetica for advertising. If you can't or won't use software that embeds your own fonts into the web page, at least use Cascading Style Sheets with fonts made for the screen, such as Verdana and Georgia, or bitmap fonts like these.

HEADLINE: VERDANA
TEXT: TENACITY CONDENSED & COND. BOLD

If time be of all things the most precious, wasting time must be the greatest prodigality; |

since lost time is never found again, | and what we call time enough always proves little enough. | Let us then be up and doing, and doing to a purpose,

so by diligence we should do more with less perplexity. | Sloth makes all things difficult, but industry all things easy. |

He that riseth late must trot all day and shall scarce overtake the business at night; while laziness travels so slowly

that poverty soon overtakes him. | Sloth, like rust, consumes faster than labor wears, while the used key is always bright. | Do not squander

time, for that's the stuff life is made of; for how much more than is necessary do we spend in sleep, forgetting that there will be sleeping enough in the grave.

So what signifies wishing and hoping for better times? | We may make these times better if we bestir ourselves. | Industry need not wish, and

he that lives upon hope will die fasting. | There are no gains without pains. | He that hath a trade

hath an estate. | Though you have found no treasure, nor has any rich relation left you a legacy, diligence is the mother

of good luck, and all things are given to industry.| Plow deep while sluggards sleep and you will have corn.

Although symbol sets are not, strictly speaking, actual typefaces, they are still able to depict Ben Franklin's message accurately. They are widely available and can be used for text, just like letters. In fact, our alphabet started out as pictograms, little drawings symbolizing objects, people, activities, or events.

A drawing of a skull and crossbones is internationally understood as a sign of death or (at least) danger; the arrow indicates direction or movement; a bed is a bed, signifying rest; a clock stands for time, the dollar sign for money.

Generally, symbols, signs, and dingbats are used to express an idea that would take up too much room to say in words, especially if it has to be understood by people from different cultures and therefore be written in more than one language. Airport signage is the obvious example.

It might be appropriate to substitute a symbol for a frequently used word or phrase, or just to add sparkle to the text. There are many symbol fonts available. Often a symbol can be used to good effect quite differently from the way it was intended. And if the symbol you want doesn't exist, just draw it for yourself in an illustration program.

Carta

Universal News and Commercial Pi

FF Care Pack

FF Bokka One

Letters are things,
not pictures of things.

Eric Gill (1882 –1940) was a
sculptor, carver of inscriptional
lettering, wood engraver, book
illustrator, and essayist on
cultural issues. Gill's eccentric
and controversial personal style
continues to be a much talked
about and incongruous element
in his list of considerable accom-
plishments. He designed the
typefaces Gill Sans, Perpetua,
and Joanna.

CHAPTER 6

Types of type

What do we remember about people? Without the aid of sound and scent, we have to rely on the visual data: the color of their eyes and their hair; are they tall or small, slight or heavy; do they wear glasses, have a beard or crooked teeth?

Many of these features are obscured and thus unavailable for use in identification when somebody steps into your path from the direction of the sun. All you see is a featureless outline. The more clothes this somebody wears, the more the shape is obscured. The worst case is the one illustrated here: we asked John, Paul, George, and Rita to wear hats and jackets for these photographs, and consequently had difficulty telling who was who when we looked at the prints.

But then that was the point. Typographically speaking, this would be like spelling words in capitals only and then putting a box around each letter. You would have to look at each letter individually to be able to spell the word, and there would be no help from the overall word shapes. Unfortunately, many signs that we are supposed to be able to read in passing are designed this way. But words are like faces: the more features we can see, the easier it is to tell who is who.

While we have made things difficult by only using capitals and putting those into a box, we at least used a typeface that is easy to read; the letterforms are distinct enough to be told apart, while not so individual that one has trouble reading complete words.

When we read longer text, we don't look at individual characters; we recognize whole word shapes and see what we expect to see. That's why we don't often spot typing errors. But when we are looking for something new or unknown, like the name of a place or a person, we need to look at each letter carefully. This is particularly true for checking names or numbers in telephone books or other directories. The typefaces designed for these purposes (shown on page 39) give prominence to individual characters. For text fonts, the art is creating clear, distinguishable letterforms that harmonize well in words and sentences.

The big test words in boxes are set in Myriad; below are alternative sans serif capitals.

JOHN **PAUL**
GEORGE **RITA**

GEORGE
ITC Avant Garde Gothic Demi

GEORGE
Gill Sans Bold

GEORGE
Din Bold

GEORGE
Futura Heavy

GEORGE
Thesis Sans Bold

GEORGE
Helvetica Bold

GEORGE
FF Meta Normal

Since it's polite to take off one's hat when meeting someone, we now have a chance to get a better look at our four well-mannered friends: still no faces, but different hairstyles give us better clues to their identities.

Setting the names in capitals and lower case gives each of the words a definite outline. If you look at them again, you could probably tell them apart just by the shape of the box, at least that is what your unconscious mind will do: if it sees a familiar shape, it will automatically give you the name associated with it.

The outline of a word is determined by which letters jut up from the main body and which hang down. They are called ascenders and descenders, respectively.

Research has shown that our eyes scan the top of the letters' x-heights during the normal reading process, so that is where the primary identification of each letter takes place. The brain assembles the information and compares it with the shape of the word's outline. If we had to consciously look at individual letters all the time, we would read as slowly as children who have not learned to assume a word's meaning from such minimal information.

While ascenders and descenders are vital for easy reading, they have to blend in so they don't attract attention to themselves. Typefaces with exaggerated details may look very attractive word by word, but are their own worst enemies when it comes to unimpeded reading. In typography, everything is connected to everything else; individual elements are noticeable only at the expense of the whole.

The test words on the left are set in capital and lowercase Myriad. Below are ascenders and descenders, as performed by four other typefaces.

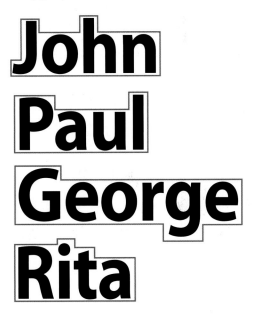

George & Paul
Antique Olive (hardly any ascenders or descenders)

George & Paul
ITC Garamond Book
(not very explicit)

George & Paul
Stempel Garamond (average)

George & Paul
Weiss Italic
(pretty obvious ascenders)

The moment of truth, in life as in typography: no more hiding behind hats or coming in from the light. Now we can look at features – eyes, lips, hair – as well as stylistic additions like glasses and haircuts. And our friends have expressions on their faces, although they were all told to look "normal."

Obviously that meant something different to each of them, as it does when typefaces are described as normal, useful, or sturdy, let alone beautiful, delicate, or handsome.

Most graphic designers and typographers agree that only a handful of typefaces is needed for their daily work; fortunately (at least for the manufacturers and type designers), they could never agree on the same dozen or so typefaces. We need thousands. Then each of us can pick our favorites. Just like shoes: one doesn't need more than half a dozen pairs, but another person will make a different selection, and so on. For individual expression, as well as maximum legibility, we need to pull out all the stops.

Picking the right font for a particular message can be fun, but also extremely difficult. What do you want to express besides the bare facts? How much do you want to interpret, add your own comment, decorate, illustrate? Even if you choose what might be called a "neutral" typeface, you've made a choice that tells people the message is neutral.

When you design the visual appearance of a message, you are adding some interpretation to it. John, Paul, George, and Rita would doubtless have a lively discussion about the typefaces chosen to represent their names and thus, them.

The choices were governed not so much by trying to get across their personalities, as by the actual letters appearing in their names. The choice of a typeface can manipulate the meaning of that word.

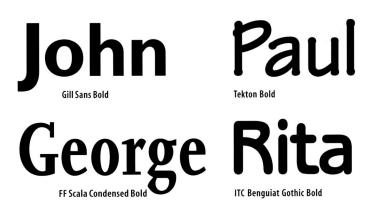

John
Gill Sans Bold

Paul
Tekton Bold

George
FF Scala Condensed Bold

Rita
ITC Benguiat Gothic Bold

It is one thing to pick typefaces to represent individual people, and quite another to express similarities as well as differences within the same family. We know that sisters and brothers don't always get along with each other. However, it is easy to tell when people belong to the same family; some take after the father, some after the mother, and some have a combination of both parents' features.

Type also comes in families. While some weights might be used more extensively than others (you wouldn't set a whole book in semibold type), there is no paternal or maternal dominance within typographic families. Each member does its work regardless of age or status. In some respects, the world of type is an ideal one.

The Von Trapp family demonstrated old-fashioned family values: live together, sing together.

Traditionally, typefaces used for setting books had no bold weights, let alone extrabold or condensed versions, or even real display weights. Those more eye-catching additions came about at the beginning of the nineteenth century, when the Industrial Revolution created the need to advertise goods.

Properly applied, however, a complete family gives you enough scope to solve all typographic problems in the setting of text. Nowadays, semibold or bold weights are part of even the most traditional families.

If you find that incestuous typography won't solve your communication problem, you can go outside and bring in some fresh blood from other families. These days, this is quite permissible – more about that on page 109.

The Adobe Garamond family was designed in 1989 by Robert Slimbach. Without its small capitals, and bold and italic children, and its titling cousin, this typographic family wouldn't be large enough to form a choir.

.Handgloves
ADOBE GARAMOND REGULAR

.*Handgloves*
ADOBE GARAMOND ITALIC

.**Handgloves**
ADOBE GARAMOND SEMIBOLD

.***Handgloves***
ADOBE GARAMOND SEMIBOLD ITALIC

.**Handgloves**
ADOBE GARAMOND BOLD

.***Handgloves***
ADOBE GARAMOND BOLD ITALIC

.HANDGLOVES
ADOBE GARAMOND TITLING

.HANDGLOVES
ADOBE GARAMOND EXPERT

Can you tell the difference between a National steel guitar, a square-neck Hawaiian, a Fender Telecaster, a Dreadnought, or an acoustic twelve-string? Look to your left. All of those guitars are there, displayed in the living room of the musician who let us take this photograph. To play a wide variety of music, all of these guitars are used.

Even though only serious musicians could detect the difference between instruments on a recording, the guitarist still has to decide which one will make the particular piece sound perfect, just as a chef will use spices you've never heard of to make your supper taste wonderful. It's the adaptation of one basic, popular tool to serve many different purposes, and the professional needs all the choices available.

When it comes to refinement, type is no exception. Not surprisingly, the fonts providing that extra something are called "expert sets." Some of them do indeed require an expert to find all the right characters and put them in the proper place, but when you have a complex problem to solve, you cannot expect a simple solution.

Remember the typewriter? It has fewer keys than a computer keyboard, and the most you could get on your golfball or daisywheel were 96 characters. Considering that the English alphabet only has 26 letters, that isn't bad, but compare it with the full character set of around 220 characters in a typical digital font.

There are languages other than English, measurements other than inches, feet, and yards. Specialized professions and sciences require their own ways of encoding and decoding messages, and expert sets make this a little easier. Two types of characters that used to be part of standard typeface families are now found in expert sets: old style figures and ligatures.

Numerals can be an eyesore when they are set in the middle of regular text. Old style figures, sometimes called lowercase figures, are endowed with features like ascenders and descenders, which allow them to blend right in with the other words on a page. Sometimes, a letter collides with a part of a neighboring one. The most obvious example is the overhang on the f and the dot on the i. Combination characters, called ligatures, prevent that unhappy collision.

fi fl ff ffi ffl

fi fl ff ffi ffl

Left: Before and after ligatures.

Right: Expert fonts are available for many popular and practical typefaces; this increases their usefulness beyond everyday jobs. Adobe Expert sets include small capitals, fractions, ligatures, special characters, and old style figures.

ABCDEFGHIJKLMN OPQRSTUVWXY&Z

¼ ½ ⅛ ⅜ ⅝ ⅔

ff fi ffi ffl fl

Å ž ý Rp ¢ $ ^ .. ý

1234567890

What if some members of your family can't sing? What if you need two sopranos, but only have one sister? Maybe you have three sisters and two brothers who can't sing or play an instrument. OK, then find yourself some outsiders, put them in the same sort of outfits, call them a "family" and everybody will believe you've been together all your lives. This is what Lawrence Welk did.

The typographic equivalent does not appear quite so harmonious. In fact, the idea is to bring in outside fonts which do things your basic family can't. Usually this means a few more heavy weights if you're setting text in a classic book typeface that hasn't got a bold, let alone an extrabold weight. Or you might need more contrast – magazine pages all set in one kind of type tend to look very gray. And then, some types look better in certain sizes, so this too has to be considered if you have text that has to be set much smaller or larger.

High-fashion designers call these things *accessoires*, and typographic equivalents have to be chosen the same way: they have to fulfill a particular function while achieving an aesthetic balance with the main dress.

The best way to add typographic impact is to use extended typeface families such as Lucida, which include a sans serif and a serif; or a family such as ITC Stone, which has a sans serif, a serif, and an informal version.

Agfa Rotis, designed in 1989 by Otl Aicher, one of Germany's best-known designers, comes in four versions: Sans, Semisans, Semiserif, and Serif.

ITC Officina was originally intended to be used for office correspondence; with a sans and serif version to be used instead of Letter Gothic or Courier.

A more daring way to add contrast and adventure to a typographic page is to invite members from other typeface families. It is generally all right to mix different types from the same designer (Eric Gill's Joanna and Gill Sans work well together, as do most of Adrian Frutiger's types), or from the same period, or even very different periods. There are almost as many recipes as there are fonts. The pages in this book are themselves examples of mixing different typefaces: Minion for text; and Myriad, a sans serif in a bold weight at a smaller size (and in another color) for sidebars, and another weight for captions.

.Handgloves
AGFA ROTIS SANS SERIF

.Handgloves
AGFA ROTIS SEMISANS

.Handgloves
AGFA ROTIS SEMISERIF

.Handgloves
AGFA ROTIS SERIF

.Handgloves
ITC OFFICINA BOOK

.*Handgloves*
ITC OFFICINA ITALIC

.**Handgloves**
ITC OFFICINA BOLD

.Handgloves
ITC OFFICINA SERIF BOOK

.*Handgloves*
ITC OFFICINA SERIF ITALIC

.**Handgloves**
ITC 117OFFICINA SERIF BOLD

.Handgloves
JOANNA REGULAR

.**Handgloves**
JOANNA EXTRA BOLD

.Handgloves
GILL SANS REGULAR

.*Handgloves*
GILL SANS REGULAR ITALIC

.**Handgloves**
GILL SANS BOLD

.*Handgloves*
GILL SANS BOLD ITALIC

Now that we've begun the music/type comparison, let's use one more example from that world to illustrate another typographic feature.

There is loud music and quiet music, dulcet tones and heavy ones, and there is – did you ever doubt it? – a typographic parallel. Some typefaces are loud by design, some are rather fine and sweet. A good family of fonts will cater to all these moods.

To illustrate the widest possible range within one family, we've chosen a typeface of many weights and versions, Helvetica, beginning with the lightest weights to suggest the tones of a flute. Very light typefaces are for those messages we want to look delicate and elegant.

Helvetica is not the most elegant type design of all time, but it is practical and neutral, and it is seen everywhere. Designed by Max Miedinger in 1957, the family grew in leaps and bounds with different typefoundries (Haas in Switzerland, Stempel and Linotype in Germany) adding weights as their customers created the demand for them. The result was a large family that didn't look very related.

When digital type became the production standard, Linotype decided to reissue the entire Helvetica family, this time coordinating all the versions to cover as many weights and widths as possible. To help distinguish among the fifty of them, they were given the same numbering system as the one originally devised by Adrian Frutiger for Univers (and since revised, as two digits were not enough to explain all the variants – see page 85); here the lightest weight is designated by a "2" in its name. The typeface has been renamed Neue (German for "new") Helvetica.

H	H	H	H	H	H	H	H
25	26	35	36	45	46	55	56

The flute makes light, delicate sounds; at the other end of the musical spectrum is the tuba with its undeniably substantial sound. As every music lover knows, a big instrument doesn't always need to be played at full volume, and a tuba will never work in the confines of a small chamber ensemble.

There are also limits to the use of very bold typefaces. At small sizes the spaces inside bold letters start filling in, making most words illegible. So, like writing music for the tuba, the best thing for bold faces is to use them where you need to accentuate rhythm and lend emphasis to the other instruments and voices.

As letters get bolder, the white space inside them decreases, making them appear smaller than lighter counterparts. The type designer allows for this effect by slightly increasing the height of bolder letters. A similar thing occurs with the width of the letter – as the thickness of the stems increases, weight is added to the outsides of the letters, making the bolder weights wider than their lighter cousins.

By the time letters are very bold, they're usually called black or heavy, or even extra black or ultra black. There is no system for naming weights in a family, so for clear communication it is safer to use the number designations when talking about a large family like Neue Helvetica.

Once the weight of a letter has reached a certain critical mass and width, it begins to look extended, as well as extra bold. Extending a design adds white space to the counters (the space inside letters), so some extended black versions may appear lighter than their narrower black counterparts.

In the case of Neue Helvetica, there is one more weight beyond the 95 (black) version: 107, extra black condensed. If you look very closely you will notice, however, that the width of its stems is no greater than those of the black weight. Condensing letter shapes makes the internal spaces smaller and the type much darker.

.**Handgloves**

65 Neue Helvetica Medium

.**Handgloves**

75 Neue Helvetica Bold

.**Handgloves**

85 Neue Helvetica Heavy

.**Handgloves**

95 Neue Helvetica Black

.**Handgloves**

107 Neue Helvetica
Extra Black Condensed

HHHHHHHHH

| 65 | 66 | 75 | 76 | 85 | 86 | 95 | 96 | 107 |

HHHHHHHHHHHH

23 24   33   34   43   44   53   54   63   64   83   84

Rhythm and contrast keep coming up when discussing good music and good typographic design. They are concepts that also apply to spoken language, as anyone who has had to sit through a monotonous lecture will attest; the same tone, volume, and speed of speech will put even the most interested listener into dreamland. Every now and again the audience needs to be shaken, either by a change in voice or pitch, by a question being posed, or by the speaker talking very quietly and then suddenly shouting. An occasional joke also works, just as the use of a funny typeface can liven up a page.

There's only one thing worse than a badly told joke, and that is a joke told twice. Whatever typographic device you come up with, don't let it turn into a gimmick. A well-coordinated range of fonts will give you the scope for contrast as well as rhythm, and will keep you secure in the bosom of a well-behaved family.

Unlike Univers, Neue Helvetica does not have extremely condensed weights, but within the traditional family of Helveticas there are dozens of other versions, from Helvetica Inserat to compressed or even extra and ultra compressed weights.

Changing the typographic rhythm by the occasional use of a condensed or, indeed, extended typeface can work wonders. Remember, however, that space problems should never be solved by setting lengthy copy in a very condensed face.

Although large families such as Helvetica can make your typographic life easy, it won't be long before they become predictable; the proverb "Jack of all trades, master of none" comes to mind. One would be foolish to ignore the special fonts that have been developed to solve particular problems.

If you want ultimate variety within one formal framework, just turn the page.

. Handgloves
HELVETICA INSERAT

. Handgloves
HELVETICA COMPRESSED

. Handgloves
HELVETICA EXTRA COMPRESSED

. Handgloves
HELVETICA ULTRA COMPRESSED

HHHHHHHHHHHHHHH

37 38 47 48 57 58 67 68 77 78 87 88 97 98 107 108

You can have as many bands, groups, combos, quartets, and quintets as you like, but nothing surpasses a full orchestra when it comes to producing all the sounds a composer can dream up. Generally, orchestra musicians use instruments that have remained largely unchanged for several hundred years; however, nowadays the odd modern instrument might be included. Again, all a little like typography. The instruments (our letters) have been around in very much the same shape for several hundred years, and the tunes (our language) haven't changed beyond recognition either. For classical page designs, we have traditional typefaces and our tried and true ways of arranging them on the page. Even new, experimental layouts work well with those types, just as modern composers can realize most of their works with a classical orchestra.

Multiple master typefaces, however, take this comparison one large step further and essentially redefine the way we use typefaces. No more static, prescribed weights and versions, but a nearly unlimited choice of typographic expression within the same framework.

These typefaces are called multiple masters because two or more sets of master designs are integrated into each typeface. These master designs determine what is known as the dynamic range of each design axis. The intermediate font variations are generated by on-demand interpolation between the master designs. For example, a light and a black master design delineate the range of possible font variations along the weight axis; you can select a font weight anywhere within this range and then "create" the font variation you choose.

A multiple master typeface can have several design axes, including weight, width, style, and optical size (see the next spread). Myriad, the first multiple master typeface, has a width as well as a weight axis, so it can be interpolated between condensed and extended, as well as between light and black. The dynamic range, therefore, extends (no pun intended) from Light Condensed to Black Semi-extended.

Check the settings on pages 140 and 141 for the application of Multiple Master technology.

A simple multiple master design matrix. The four corners represent the master designs.

Ergonomics can be defined as the study of the dynamic interaction between people and their environments, or as the science that seeks to adapt working conditions to better suit the worker. People suffer if chairs are too low, tables too high, lights too dim, or if computer screens have too little contrast or emit too much radiation.

Children could tell stories about having to sit at adult tables, clutching forks that are far too big for them and having to drink from glasses they cannot get their little hands around.

This is similar to what has been done to many typefaces since the introduction of the pantograph in the late 1800s; the practice became even more prevalent with the advent of photo-typesetting in the mid-1960s. One size had to fit all. One master drawing was used to generate everything, from very small type to headline-size type and beyond. The multiple master optical size axis makes it possible to bring out the variations in design details that allow a typeface to be optimized for readability at different sizes.

Typographic ergonomics at last.

When type was made out of metal (see page 55), each size had to be designed differently and cut separately. The engraver knew from experience what had to be done to make each size highly readable. On very small type, hairlines were a little heavier so they would not only be easier to read, but also not break under pressure from the printing press.

When one master design is used to fit all sizes, as in photo-typesetting and digital systems, these subtleties are lost, resulting in compromises that very often give type designs a bad name. This is especially true of the re-creations of classic faces: as originally designed, the types permitted only a limited range of sizes acceptable in terms of readability and aesthetics.

Minion multiple master has an optical size axis that makes it possible to generate fonts that are optically adjusted for use at specific point sizes: the text sizes are clear and easy to read, and display sizes are refined and elegant.

Minion multiple master was designed in 1991 by Robert Slimbach, who was inspired by old style typefaces of the late Renaissance. You can form your own opinion of this type and its italic companion, as well as its expert set, by looking at the main text in this book.

Hmfg
6-point

Hmfg
72-point

Compare the differences between the letter shapes and overall weight of the above letters. The 6-point design has heavier stems and serifs, wider characters, and a larger x-height.

When this book first came out, computer screens looked and worked very much like TV sets. Flat screens were desirable but seemed unobtainable and too expensive. Today, CRT monitors look almost ridiculous. Flat LCD screens not only offer higher resolution, but the technology also allowed engineers to come up with more tricks to make bitmaps look acceptable to our eyes. Adobe has developed *CoolType*, which uses color anti-aliasing. On old monitors, only whole pixels could be manipulated, but on digital LCD screens, *CoolType* controls the smaller red, green, and blue subpixels, individually adjusting their intensity. This effectively trebles the horizontal grid and achieves more precise smoothing along the edges of characters. A similar technology from Microsoft is called *ClearType*. It may take another few generations of engineers and programmers to achieve the typographic quality we've been acustomed to for over 500 years.

Our experience with print shapes our expectations for other media. To make type on screens look acceptable to our physical requirements and cultural expectations, type designers now have to enlist the help of engineers and programmers. They fit unwieldy bitmaps into strict grids, then instruct the pixels to only appear in certain desired positions, and finally add gray pixels to the jagged outlines to makes us see smooth curves where there are only coarse pixels. It takes quite a bit of effort to overcome the inherent deficiencies of digital media.

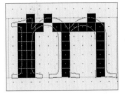

This is what happens when pixels try to fill outlines – some stems are wider than others and details, such as serifs, disappear.

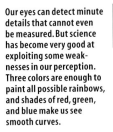

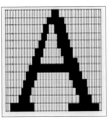

Our eyes can detect minute details that cannot even be measured. But science has become very good at exploiting some weaknesses in our perception. Three colors are enough to paint all possible rainbows, and shades of red, green, and blue make us see smooth curves.

pack my box with
dog effect coffin :
wyvern foxy syry
Of the greatest ar
look with too mu

pack my box wit
dog effect coffin
wyvern foxy syr
Of the greatest a
look with too mu

typography

typography

Shades of gray make curves and diagonals appear smooth; this sample is enlarged from a small bitmap.

Hinting – the instruction of bitmaps to appear in regular, predetermined positions only – overcomes irregular letter shapes and random spacing.

Anyone who would letterspace
lower case would steal sheep.

Frederic Goudy (1865–1947),
American typographer and type
designer, did not design his first
typeface until he was forty-five.
He is noted for his profusion of
innovative and eclectic type
designs and his forthright
declarations on typographic
issues.

CHAPTER 7

How it works

Letters were originally invented to help communicate not high culture, but mundane things like the amount of goods delivered or their value in barter or currency. What began as individual signs representing real items developed into letters and alphabets. Different cultures added to the typographic variety. For instance, the most common vowel sound in an ancient language was also the the first letter of its alphabet. The Phoenicians (ca. 1000 B.C.) called it *aleph*, the Greeks (ca. 500 B.C.), *alpha*, the Romans (ca. 50 B.C.), *ah*. The Phoenicians had twenty-two letters in their alphabet; the Greeks added vowels, and the Romans developed the letters we still use today. All this time, people wrote either from right to left, or left to right, or top to bottom.

Tree farms are to forests what monospaced fonts are to real type.

With such a mixed history, no wonder our alphabet looks so unbalanced. Anyone inventing a new alphabet today would doubtless be more practical and make letters more regular. There would be more obvious differences between some shapes, and no narrow letters such as *l* in the same alphabet with wide ones such as *m*.

One consequence of our letters having such complex yet delicate shapes is that we have to respect their space. Every one of them needs enough room on both sides to avoid clashes with its neighbors. The smaller the type, the more space that's needed on the sides. Only big, robust headlines can support the occasional very closely spaced letters.

The history of type is a history of technical constraints. Mechanical typewriters gave us monospaced fonts. Each letter had the same amount of lateral space, regardless of its shape. Later developments led to typewriter fonts with more regular letter shapes; this did not necessarily improve legibility, but these newer alphabets no longer had any gaps between characters. They also appear extremely readable to computers, who don't care that much about tradition.

As soon as typewriters got little computers inside them, they were able to set justified text (lines of the same length), a style which was, and is, largely unnecessary in office communication. But people had learned from reading newspapers, magazines, and books that this was how type should be set.

Now technology allows us to typeset most of the alphabets ever created and actually improve on their appearance, definition, and arrangement. Proportionately spaced fonts are easier to read, occupy less space, allow for more expression, and are nicer to look at. There are only two reasons to still use monospaced fonts: to imitate the time-honored and personal look of typewriters and to write plain text emails (see page 169).

Himdgloves

Himdgloves

In monospaced typewriter typefaces, every letter occupies the same lateral space: the *i* is stretched on the rack, while the *m* suffers claustrophobia. The most common measurements are 12 characters to the inch (elite) or 10 to the inch (pica).

Looking at nature, we imagine that God could have designed more practical forests than the ones we know: they are difficult to get around in, full of different kinds of trees in various stages of growth, and there's not enough light. Luckily, we humans are also part of this wonderful, if not entirely perfect, system called nature; we like things that look "human" (less than perfect), but we also like that things conform to a master plan, even if it is indecipherable. We know when something looks "right" without ever having to measure it.

Unfortunately, people have long since begun improving on creation. We won't go into a discussion of inventions like nuclear power or low-fat dog food, but certainly tree farms are a good example of what some people think nature should look like. If we applied the same logic to type, we wouldn't have any unusual or eccentric designs, where every letter has a different shape and its own individual space. Instead there would only be regularized fonts with nice geometrically defined shapes. How mundane our typographic lives would be.

There are sometimes unsightly gaps that occur between and around particular combinations of letters. Obvious problem letters are *V*, *W*, and *Y* in both capitals and lower case. Other bad gaps appear between numerals and periods or commas, particularly after a 7. (Just like this.)

Once you look into the relationship of two or more characters in a word, you realize what a mess it can be – not unlike other relationships. One of the most often-spoken words in desktop typography makes its appearance at this point: *kerning*. To get rid of these gaps, one simply removes space (or maybe adds it) between the offending pair of letters. A certain number of these problem combinations are adjusted by the type designer; they are known as "kerning pairs" and are included in font programs.

Tracking controls the space between letters globally; this means that equal amounts of space can be added between every letter in your text. It is here that Mr. Goudy's dictum reminds us of the impending danger: as the space between letters increases, so does the difficulty comprehending single words, and thus the thought conveyed in the text.

Unsightly character combinations are remedied with kerning.

To Tr Ve Wo

BEFORE KERNING

To Tr Ve Wo

AFTER KERNING

r. y, 7. w -

BEFORE KERNING

r. y, 7. w-

AFTER KERNING

Letters, like trees, hardly ever appear by themselves. As soon as a bunch of letters are gathered together, they fight for space, for the right to be recognized, to be read. If you plant trees too close to each other, they'll struggle to get light and for space for their roots to expand; the weaker ones will stop growing and eventually die.

Before this turns into a tale of typographic Darwinism, let's look at the practical consequences as far as this book and its subject is concerned. If you know your text is going to be fairly long and that it will require some time to read, you should adjust the layout accordingly. The lines should be long enough to get complete thoughts into them and there ought to be enough space between them to allow readers to finish reading a line before their eye gets distracted by the next.

Marathon runners know they have twenty-six miles ahead of them, so it would be foolish to start off like crazy. There is also no need to run in narrow tracks, since by the time everybody gets settled into the race there will be plenty of room, with the first runners miles away from the last ones. With thousands of people in the race, individuals will blend into the crowd, but they still have to give their best.

Long texts need to be read the way a marathon is run. Everything has to be comfortable – once you've found your rhythm, nothing must disturb it again. If you have text that is going to require long-distance reading, design it so the reader has a chance to settle in. The rhythm depends on the spacing contingencies below.

Letters need to be far enough apart to be distinct from one another, but not so far that they separate into individual, un-related signs. Mr. Goudy knew what he was talking about.

Word spaces have to be gauged so that the reader is able to see individual words, but can also group them together for quick comprehension.

The space between lines of type has to be generous enough to prevent the eye from slipping to the next line before it is finished gathering information in the current one.

The text below has been set for comfortable long-distance reading.

If time be of all things the most precious, wasting time must be the greatest prodigality; since lost time is never found again, and what we call time enough always proves little enough. Let us then be up and doing, and doing to a purpose, so by diligence we should do more with less perplexity. Sloth makes all things difficult, but industry all things easy. He that riseth late must trot all day and shall scarce overtake the business at night; while laziness travels so slowly that poverty soon overtakes him. Sloth, like rust, consumes faster than labor wears, while the used key is always bright. Do not squander time, for that's the stuff life is

What did people do before there was the instant replay? A 100-yard dash is over in less than ten seconds these days, and spectators can't possibly look at each of the six or more contestants by the time they're across the line. Does that bring to mind the experience of thumbing through a magazine, with all those ads flashing by your eyes in split seconds? That's typography at its most intense. If you want to make an impression in an ad, you can't wait for readers to get settled in, and there is no space to spread your message out in front of their eyes. The sprinter has to hurl forward, staying in a narrow lane. In short-distance text, lines must be short and compact or the reader's eye will be drawn to the next line before reaching the end of its predecessor.

Setting text in short lines for quick scanning requires rearrangement of all the other parameters, too. Tracking can be tighter, and word spaces and line spaces smaller.

The choice of typefaces is, of course, another consideration. A type that invites you to read long copy has to be inconspicuous and self-effacing, confirming our acquired prejudices about what is readable. A quick look at a short piece of writing could be assisted by a typeface that has a little verve. It shouldn't be as elaborate as a display font used on a label or a poster, but it also doesn't need to be too modest.

If time be of all things the most precious, wasting time must be the greatest prodigality; since lost time is never found again, and what we call time enough always proves little enough. Let us then be up and doing, and doing to a purpose, so by diligence we should do more with less perplexity. Sloth makes all things difficult, but industry all things easy. He that riseth late must trot all day and shall scarce overtake the business at night; while laziness travels so slowly that poverty soon overtakes him. Sloth, like rust, consumes faster than labor wears, while the used key is always bright. Do not squander time, for that's the stuff life is made of; how much more than is necessary do we spend in sleep, forgetting that the sleeping fox catches no poultry, and that there will be sleeping enough in the grave. So what signifies wishing and hoping for better times?

The above text has been tuned for sprint reading. Compare the long-distance text from the previous page.

While driving on freeways isn't quite as exhausting as running a marathon (mainly because you get to sit down in your car), it requires a similar mindset. The longer the journey, the more relaxed your driving style should be. You know you're going to be on the road for a while, and it's best not to get too nervous, but sit back, keep a safe distance from the car in front of you, and cruise.

Long-distance reading needs a relaxed attitude, too. There is nothing worse than having to get used to a different set of parameters every other line: compare it with the jarring effect of a fellow motorist who suddenly appears in front of you, having jumped a lane just to gain twenty yards. Words should also keep a safe, regular distance from each other, so that you can rely on the next one to appear when you're ready for it.

The tricky thing about space is that it is generally invisible and therefore easy to ignore. At night you can see only as far as the headlights of your car can shine. You determine your speed by the size of the visible space in front of you.

It used to be a rule of thumb for headline settings to leave a space between words that is just wide enough to fit in a lowercase *i*. For comfortable reading of long lines, the space between words should be much wider.

The default settings in most software vary these values, but the normal 100 percent word space seems just fine for lines of at least ten words (or just over fifty characters). Shorter lines always require tighter word space (more about that on the following page spread).

Theiwayitoiwealth

Iftimebeofallthings
themostprecious,wasting
timemustbethegreatest
prodigality;sincelosttimeis
neverfoundagain,andwhat
wecalltimeenoughalways
proveslittleenough.Letus
thenbeupanddoing,and
doingtoapurpose,sobydili-
genceweshoulddomore

Iftimebeofallthings
themostprecious,wasting
timemustbethegreatest
prodigality;sincelosttimeis
neverfoundagain,andwhat
wecalltimeenoughalways
proveslittleenough.Letus
thenbeupanddoing,and
doingtoapurpose,sobydili-
genceweshoulddomorewith

A lowercase *i* makes a nice word space for headlines. Short lines should have modest space between the words.

You must have noticed that the lanes on the freeway are wider than those on city streets, even though cars of the same size use both types of road. This is because when traveling at high speeds, every movement of the steering wheel can cause a major deviation from the lane you're supposed to be driving in, posing a threat to other drivers.

This is, in typographic terms, not the space between words, but that between lines – the lanes that words "drive" in. Typographic details and refinement relate to everything else; if you increase your word spacing, you have to have more space between the lines as well.

One rule to remember about line space is that it needs to be larger than the space between words, otherwise your eye would be inclined to travel from the word on the first line directly to the word on the line below. When line space is correct, your eye will make the journey along one line before it continues on to the next.

The rest is very simple: the more words per line, the more space needed between the lines. You can then increase the space *ever so slightly* between the letters (that is, track them) as the lines get longer.

If time be of all things the most precious, wasting time must be the greatest prodigality; since lost time is never found again, and what we call time enough always proves little enough. Let us then be up and doing, and doing to a purpose, so by diligence we should do more with less perplexity. Sloth makes all things difficult, but industry all things easy. He that riseth late must trot all day and shall scarce overtake the business at night; while laziness travels so slowly that poverty soon overtakes him. Sloth, like rust, consumes faster than labor wears, while the used key is always bright. Do not squander time, for that's the stuff life is made of; how much more than is necessary do we spend in sleep, forgetting that the sleeping fox catches no poultry, and that there will be sleeping enough in the grave. So what signifies wishing and hoping for better times? We may make these times better if we bestir ourselves. Industry need not wish, and he that lives upon hope will die fasting. There are no gains without pains. He that has a trade has an estate, and he that has a calling has an office of profit and honor. But then the trade must be worked at and the calling honored. But then the trade

The miracle of computers has enabled line spaces to be adjusted in very small increments. In this example, none

of the other parameters has changed – tracking and word space remain the same, but the line space increases.

Notice how the more widely spaced lines cry out for looser tracking and wider word spaces.

In both driving and typography, the object is to get safely and quickly from A to B. What is safe at sixty miles an hour on a straight freeway with four lanes in good daylight would be suicide in city traffic. You have to adjust your driving to the road conditions, and you have to adjust typographic parameters to the conditions of the page and the purpose of the message.

Whether you're driving along looking at the scenery, or stuck in a traffic jam, or slowly moving from one set of lights to the next, you have to be conscious of the drivers around you. If they change their behavior, you have to react. When you learn the rules and have had a little practice, nothing will upset you, not in traffic and not in typography.

One of the best ways to keep the reader's attention on the content of your message is to keep the color of the printed text consistent. Newspapers do a very bad job of it. They agree that type, even in narrow columns, has to be justified. The result is words and lines that are erratically letterspaced. Readers have become used to that style (or rather, lack of it); loose and tight lines of type, one after another, don't seem to upset anyone.

In other surroundings, however, lines that look a little lighter and then a little darker because no one has adjusted the spacing might make the reader think there is some purpose behind this arrangement: are the loose lines more important than the tight ones?

Again, and there is no guarantee this is the last time: every time you change one spacing parameter, you have to look closely at all the others and adjust them accordingly.

If time be of all things the most precious, wasting time must be the greatest prodigality; since lost time is never found again, and what we call time enough always proves little enough. Let us then be up and doing, and doing to a purpose, so by diligence we should

If time be of all things the most precious, wasting time must be the greatest prodigality; since lost time is never found again, and what we call time enough always proves little enough. Let us then be up and doing, and doing to a purpose, so by diligence we should do more with less perplexity.

If time be of all things the most precious, wasting time must be the greatest prodigality; since lost time is never found again, and what we call time enough always proves little enough. Let us then be up and doing, and doing to a purpose, so by diligence we should do more with less perplexity. Sloth makes all

Longer lines need wider spaces: in these examples, line space, tracking, and word spaces have all been increased as the lines were widened.

There are situations, and this really is the final car picture, in which normal rules don't apply. Space becomes a rare commodity indeed when thousands of people are trying to get to the same place at the same time. Some pages are just like a downtown traffic jam: too many messages, too many directions, and too much noise.

One thing typography can do, however, that city planning cannot: we can make all of our vehicles different sizes, move them up and down, overlap them, put them into the background, or turn them sideways. A page like this looks better than your typical downtown gridlock.

Space

Traffic
Traffic Traffic Traffic
Traffic
Traffic Traffi Traffic
Traffic Traffic
Traffi Traffic Traffic
Traffic
Traffic Traffic
Traffic Traffic
Overlap Overlap
Overlap Overlap
Overlap
Traffic
Sideways
Traffic
Gridlock
Gridlock Gridlocks
Gridlock Gridlock Gridlock
Gridlock Gridlock
Gridlock Gridlock Gridlock
Gridlock

Perspective

Background
Background
Background
Background Background
BackgroundBackground Background
Background Background
BackgroundBackground BackgroundBackground
BackgroundBackground BackgroundBackground
BackgroundBackground BackgroundBackground
BackgroundBackground BackgroundBackground
Foreground
Foreground
dbackground ound
ound
BackgroundBackground
ound
undBackground

If time be of all things the most precious, wasting time must be the greatest prodigality; since lost time is never found again, and what we call time enough always proves little enough. Let us then be up and doing, and doing to a purpose, so by diligence we should do more with less perplexity. Sloth makes all things difficult, but industry all things easy. He that riseth late must trot all day and shall scarce overtake the business at night; while laziness travels so slowly that poverty soon overtakes him. Sloth, like rust, consumes faster than labor wears, while the used key is always bright.

This copy is set to the same specifications as the second example on page 141, but reversed out.

If time be of all things the most precious, wasting time must be the greatest prodigality; since lost time is never found again, and what we call time enough always proves little enough. Let us then be up and doing, and doing to a purpose, so by diligence we should do more with less perplexity. Sloth makes all things difficult, but industry all things easy. He that riseth late must trot all day and shall scarce overtake the business at night; while laziness travels so slowly that poverty soon overtakes him. Sloth, like rust, consumes faster than labor wears, while the used key is always bright.

In reversed-out settings, the spaces between letters look smaller, because they are dark. This text is set with the letterspacing (tracking) more open than in the example above.

If time be of all things the most precious, wasting time must be the greatest prodigality; since lost time is never found again, and what we call time enough always proves little enough. Let us then be up and doing, and doing to a purpose, so by diligence we should do more with less perplexity. Sloth makes all things difficult, but industry all things easy. He that riseth late must trot all day and shall scarce overtake the business at night; while laziness travels so slowly that poverty soon overtakes him. Sloth, like rust, consumes faster than labor wears, while the used key is always bright.

White type looks heavier than black type (dark color recedes, bright colors come forward), so we created an instance of Minion multiple master that was lighter in weight.

If time be of all things the most precious, wasting time must be the greatest prodigality; since lost time is never found again, and what we call time enough always proves little enough. Let us then be up and doing, and doing to a purpose, so by diligence we should do more with less perplexity. Sloth makes all things difficult, but industry all things easy. He that riseth late must trot all day and shall scarce overtake the business at night; while laziness travels so slowly that poverty soon overtakes him. Sloth, like rust, consumes faster than labor wears, while the used key is always bright.

Often the problem is not that white type looks too heavy, but that the ink-spread from the printing process fills in the open spaces in and around letters. We have chosen a smaller optical size of Minion multiple master to make it a little sturdier.

1

If time be of all things the most precious, wasting time must be the greatest prodigality; since lost time is never found again, and what we call time enough always proves little enough. Let us then be up and doing, and doing to a purpose, so by diligence we should do more with less perplexity. Sloth makes all things difficult, but industry all things easy. He that riseth late must trot all day and shall scarce overtake the business at night; while laziness travels so slowly that poverty soon overtakes him. Sloth, like rust, consumes faster than labor wears, while the used key is always bright.

Remember: the more letters contained in a line, the more space that's needed between words and lines.

2

If time be of all things the most precious, wasting time must be the greatest prodigality; since lost time is never found again, and what we call time enough always proves little enough. Let us then be up and doing, and doing to a purpose, so by diligence we should do more with less perplexity. Sloth makes all things difficult, but industry all things easy. He that riseth late must trot all day and shall scarce overtake the business at night; while laziness travels so slowly that poverty soon overtakes him. Sloth, like rust, consumes faster than labor wears, while the used key is always bright.

For comparison among the various settings, the horizontal and vertical scales are broken down into millimeter units.

3

If time be of all things the most precious, wasting time must be the greatest prodigality; since lost time is never found again, and what we call time enough always proves little enough. Let us then be up and doing, and doing to a purpose, so by diligence we should do more with less perplexity. Sloth makes all things difficult, but industry all things easy. He that riseth late must trot all day and shall scarce overtake the business at night; while laziness travels so slowly that poverty soon overtakes him. Sloth, like rust, consumes faster than labor wears, while the used key is always bright.

If time be of all things the most precious, wasting time must be the greatest prodigality; since lost time is never found again, and what we call time enough always proves little enough. Let us then be up and doing, and doing to a purpose, so by diligence we should do more with less perplexity. Sloth makes all things difficult, but industry all things easy. He that riseth late must trot all day and shall scarce overtake the business at night; while laziness travels so slowly that poverty soon overtakes him. Sloth, like rust, consumes faster than labor wears, while the used key is always bright.

The first example has approximately 4 words (25 characters) per line and is set in 8-point type with 9-point line space (set 8 on 9); word spaces are very small and tracking is very loose. The second example accommodates 8 words (45 characters) per line, is set 8 on 8; word spaces are 10 percent wider and tracking is loose. The third block of text is set 8 on 11, with about 10 words (58 characters) to a line; the word space is opened another 10 percent, and the tracking is a little tighter. The fourth text block is set 8 on 12, and with 15 words (90 characters) per line, which is almost too wide. The word spaces are now at the default value, with a little tracking.

Symmetry is static — that is
to say quiet; that is to say,
inconspicuous.

William Addison Dwiggins
(1880 –1956) was a typographer,
type designer, puppeteer, and
author. The American book trade
owes a debt to Dwiggins for
bringing style and good design
sense into mainstream publishing, most notably with the work
he did on Borzoi Books for the
publisher, Alfred A. Knopf. He is
responsible for reintroducing
colophon pages, which give
details about a book's typography and fascinating facts about
the typefaces used. Caledonia,
Metro, and Electra are Dwiggins
typeface designs.

CHAPTER 8

Putting it to work

The bed is one piece of furniture that has escaped most design trends. Mattresses have changed and so has the technology of making bed frames, but the way we sleep is still the same and the basic bedroom looks just as it has for centuries.

Bedrooms and books have one thing in common: an essentially single purpose. Reading, like sleeping, hasn't changed much in several hundred years, although we now have reading glasses, electrically operated headrests, and little lamps that clip right onto our books.

It may be said that the forerunner of what we consider coffee table books existed in the early days of printing, showing small illustrations positioned in a narrow marginal column next to the main body of text. Paperbacks crammed full of poorly spaced type with narrow page margins are an unfortunate and fairly recent innovation. But the intimate process of reading a book remains largely unchanged, as does the look of books.

Common to every book design is the underlying grid that divides the page into areas that serve different purposes – columns of text, marginal comments, headlines, footnotes, captions, illustrations. The more complex the structure of the text, the more possibilities for the arrangement of elements supported by this grid. Linear reading (as in a novel) usually just needs a straightforward, single-column layout, for which there are plenty of successful historical precedents.

The size of a book is crucial, but it is often determined by technical or marketing constraints. Books for serious reading should fit in our hands; it is preferable, then, to have a narrow format with wide margins that allow room for fingers to hold the book.

The column width (i.e., the length of a line of type) is governed by the width of the page, the size of type, and the number of words or characters per line. One or more of these variables is usually given, or is unavoidable, simplifying the other design decisions.

Type for extended reading should be no smaller than 9 point and no larger than 14 point. Point size is a fairly arbitrary measurement (see page 55), so these suggestions are valid only for "normal" book typefaces – types with a very pronounced or very small x-height need to be carefully evaluated.

The arrangements or layouts of our living rooms still follow the same model they did generations ago. There is usually a comfortable chair or two, perhaps a sofa to accommodate more than one person, a table, a bookshelf, some lights. The only recent addition to this harmonious ensemble has been the television set, which took over the center of attention from the hearth.

Living rooms, as opposed to bedrooms, serve a multitude of functions. Families sit together, and when they're not all staring in the same direction watching TV, they might actually play games at the table, eat dinner (frequently staring in the same direction), or even pursue other interests such as reading or conversing.

Certain types of books are used the same way: you can read, browse, look at pictures, or even check on something of particular interest. Pages offer various levels of entry for readers, viewers, and occasional browsers. These books will have to look different than our time-honored tomes of linear reading, just as living rooms look different than bedrooms.

Some books look like catalogs, some like magazines. Some have the structure of a typical novel, but with illustrations, either integrated into the text or on separate pages. The reader is likely to peruse this sort of book in a more casual fashion, so the designer needs to provide several levels of distinct typographic elements to act as guides through text and images.

If it has to be larger to accommodate pictures, or to provide room for text set in multiple columns, a book most likely will have to be set down on a table to be studied rather than read. This means that the margins can be smaller (no room needed for fingers to hold it) and that pictures can even extend to the edges of pages.

While books with only one level of copy usually need only one typeface in one size plus italic and small caps, more specialized books (such as this one) have to distinguish among the main text and other elements. This could mean a pronounced difference in type size; or perhaps another typeface with contrasting design or weight, or another color. In this book, we've employed a few of these devices at the same time.

If the contents, the illustrations, and the amount of copy vary from page to page, a flexible grid is needed. The one in this book allows for many different column widths, captions, and sidebars. These elements shouldn't be changed randomly on every other page, but when they do have to be adapted to varying contents, the underlying grid structure serves as a common denominator.

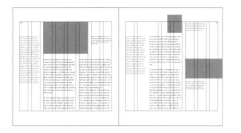

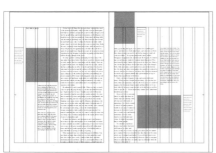

Hotel lobbies are institutional living rooms. Guests and visitors spend time there doing what they might do at home, but in the company of strangers. The dress has to be more formal and one's attention is more likely to be distracted by the things going on, and the general level of activity rules out listening to one's personal choice of music. There is still the opportunity, however, for all to sit staring in the same direction, watching TV.

Some people manage to read real books in quasi-public places like hotel lobbies, but most spend their time there waiting for someone or something, so they are only able to read magazines. Magazine pages are designed for the casual reader: there are snippets of information or gossip (or one dressed up as the other), headlines, captions, and other graphical signposts pointing toward various tidbits of copy.

As advertisements change their look according to the latest cognitive fashion, editorial pages tend to either look trendier, or to deliberately stay sober, bookish, and authoritative.

Most magazines are printed in standard sizes; in the USA this means they're close to 8 ½ by 11 inches. A line of type needs to be at least six words (between 35 and 40 characters) long, so the type ought to be about 10 point to arrive at a column width of 55 to 60 mm, or 2¼ to 2⅜ inches. Three of these columns fit onto the page, leaving acceptable margins. The three-column grid is thus the basis for most publications printed on A4 = 210 x 297 mm. 8½ x 11 inches = 216 x 279 mm.

To allow for other elements besides the main text columns, these measurements have to be divided again. Captions can be set in smaller type and in very short lines, so they might fit into half a basic column, making it a six-unit grid.

A good way to make these grids more flexible and spontaneous is to leave one wide margin that would only occasionally be filled with type. This grid would then have an odd number of units, say seven or even thirteen. The more complex the contents, the more supple the grid has to be, allowing for different stories in different-size types to occupy different widths.

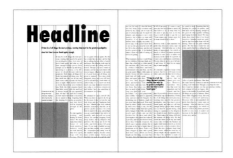

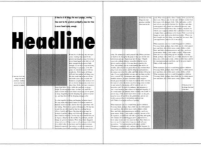

Kitchens are rooms with a clearly defined purpose: the storage, preparation, and often consumption of food and beverages. The equipment for these activities has changed considerably over the years and one could list numerous parallels to the development of typesetting systems over the same time span. The basic purpose has remained unchanged in both cases, whether it concerns food or type.

In a kitchen there are different surfaces for particular tasks, and containers and shelves for food, tools, dishes, pots, and pans. Graphic designers and typographers call the containers columns or picture boxes, the food is the text, the surface the page, and the tools are the typographic parameters needed to prepare an interesting page for the reader who has to digest it all.

Each recipe in a cookbook usually has explanatory text, a list of ingredients, and a step-by-step guide. It is sometimes illustrated either with small photographs or drawings. This sort of structure applies to any how-to publication, whether it's for car mechanics or landscapers.

People read cookbooks and other how-to manuals in situations that are often less than ideal. A cookbook has to compete for tabletop space with food, knives, towels, and bowls, and there is never enough time to read anything carefully. The text has to be read while standing, which means the type should be larger than usual. The recipe steps have to be clearly labeled with short headlines; ingredients and measurements should be in lists that can be referred to at a glance.

One of the best – or worst – examples of badly designed information is found in instructions for mounting snow chains onto the wheels of your car. This operation is usually done in the dark when you're wet, in a hurry, and uncomfortably cold. The instructions are often printed on white paper, which invariably gets wet and dirty before you've finished the job.

The typographic solution is to print them on the outside of the package, which should be made of some plastic material. The best color combination would be black type on a yellow background, which wouldn't show dirt as much as white. The type should be big and strong so it's legible no matter what. The text should be set in short, simple words and sentences.

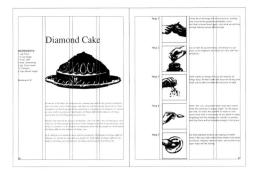

We spend much of our time outside our homes in places where our priorities are defined by other people. This is the case in most public places and, unfortunately, at work. Many people still have to work in conditions very much like this typing pool of the 1940s, even though it would be easy to improve the environment and thus the quality of work.

The same goes for much typographic work. There is no reason for hardworking pieces like price lists, technical catalogs, timetables, and similar heavy-duty information to look as ugly or complicated as they often do. If something looks dull, repetitive, and off-putting, people will approach it with a negative attitude (if they approach it at all). This does not improve their willingness to absorb the information.

Computers are a huge improvement over mechanical typewriters, and the output of laser printers certainly looks much better than anything that ever came out of a typewriter. To create good visual communication, however, takes much more than good tools. Whenever you come across those official-looking, unreadable pieces, don't blame it on the equipment.

Complex information, such as price lists and timetables, cannot be designed on a pre-conceived grid. The page arrangement has to stem from the content and structure of the information itself. First you have to find the shortest and the longest elements, and then ignore them; if your layout accommodates the extremes you will end up making allowances for a few isolated exceptions. The thing to do is to make the bulk of the matter fit, then go back to the exceptions and work with them one by one. If there are only a few long lines in an otherwise short listing, it should be considered an opportunity to flex your creative muscles: design around them or rewrite.

A sure way to improve the look and function of any information-intensive document is to eliminate boxes. Vertical lines are almost always unnecessary. Type creates its own vertical divisions along the lefthand edges of columns as long as there is sufficient space between columns. A vertical line is wasteful because it needs precious space on either side. Use space to divide elements from each other. Utilize horizontal lines to accentuate areas of the page. The edge of the paper makes its own box and doesn't require more boxes inside it.

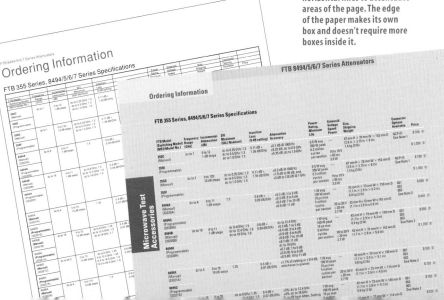

The typing pool is as old fashioned as boxes on forms. Today's "information" workers still sit at a desk and type on keyboards, but they are allowed to move around, talk to other workers, get drinks, and actually exchange information with each other. Even the office cubicle, which was the successor to the typing pool, seems on its way out. The more liberal attitudes in our work space tend to show up in our design tastes.

Many menial tasks, such as typing the same information again and again, is done via the "copy and paste" command, and programs just need one keystroke to call up previously stored information about your address and credit card numbers. The biggest problem now is to remember all your passwords without writing them down on a sticky note and displaying that on your computer screen for everyone to see.

A business that wants to attract good people and keep them motivated has to indulge them a little. Christmas lights in summer, plastic pets, or artificial palm trees are signs of a culture that judges people by work and not by strict compliance with corporate rules. Firms that design forms with lots of little boxes and redundant lines probably still keep their employees in small cubicles.

Web pages will look very different on the user's desktop than on the designer's screen unless they conform to some widespread, and therefore rather bland, standards. As one cannot expect the typical end-user to have more fonts than those that come with typical systems, main text on a web page can only use fonts such as Arial, Geneva, Verdana, Times, etc. You can, however, at least define which fonts your browser will use to fill in the fields with your personal information. For some very old reasons, PCs still only count 54 points to an inch, whereas the Mac has 72 points. This means that type on a PC looks about one-third bigger than on a Mac screen with comparable resolution. Web designers have to use software like Cascading Style Sheets to ensure users see the same layout in their browsers, irrespective of the platform.

If that is not the case, designers didn't do their job properly or you have a very old browser.

Identifier	Data	Description/Comments
First Name		
Last Name		
E-Mail address		Your E-Mail address. This must be the same as the registered Technical Contact Person in our records.
Telephone		Phone number you can be reached during working hours - If any further information is required for authentication verification. Please add full country prefix !
Fax Number		
Company Name		
Login Name		
Password		
Password		
e-Identification question		

Billing Information

Please fill out the order form below. Bold fields are required in order to complete your purchase transaction. By providing this informaton, you agree that Adobe Systems Software Ireland Limited ("Adobe") or its designee may process the information for such purpose.

Please enter your billing information exactly as it appears on your credit card statement.

First Name
erik

Last Name
spiekermann

Company

Address
motzstrasse 58

Address 2

City
berlin

Post Code
10777

Country of residence:
Germany

Email
erik@spiekermann.com

Phone

Use of Personal Information

☐ I would like to receive information and special promotions Adobe products and services.

☐ I would like to receive information and special promotions from parties other than Adobe on their products and servi

Unless you indicate otherwise in the checkboxes above, your personal information will only be used in connection with this o See our Online Privacy Policy for details on how your information may be used by Adobe Systems.

Important Information

If you reside in the European Union, please indicate your consent t the personal information you have provided may be transferred and stored in countries outside of the EU, including the United States. I you fail to provide your consent, you will not be permitted to purcha the software online.

☑ I consent

▶ CONTINUE

Now that your wife has bought you a new suit, I don't mind starting up a correspondence.

Groucho Marx (1895–1977) was a member of the Marx Brothers, one of the funniest comedy teams in movie history. In films like *Horse Feathers* and *Duck Soup,* Groucho is perpetually punning while displaying a remarkable facility for the leering look.

CHAPTER 9

There is no bad type

From Mediterranean merchants making notes on clay tablets, to Roman masons chiseling letters into stone, to medieval monks moving quills across parchment – the look of letters has always been influenced by the tools used to make them. Two hundred years ago copperplate engraving changed the look of typefaces, as did all subsequent technologies: the pantograph, Monotype and Linotype machines, phototypesetting, digital bitmaps, and outline fonts.

Most of these technologies are no longer viable, but some of the typefaces they engendered now represent particular categories of typefaces. Once again, the best example is the typewriter. As an office machine it is all but dead, but its typeface style survives as a typographic stereotype. Other recognizable typeface styles that have outlived their production methods are stenciled letters and constructed letters made with a square and compass.

Technical constraints no longer exist when it comes to the reproduction or re-creation of types from any and all periods. What used to be a necessity has become a look, just like prewashed jeans are supposed to make anybody look like a cowboy who's been out on the trail for a few months.

Designers have gotten good mileage out of the low-tech look. Theoretically, almost every typeface could be stenciled; all it takes is a few lines to connect the inside shapes to the outside so the letters won't fall apart when cut out of metal.

At almost the same time two designers had the clever idea of creating a stencil typeface. Stencil, designed by R. Hunter Middleton, was released in June of 1937; in July of that same year, Stencil, designed by Gerry Powell, was debuted.

Today anybody can potentially make a typeface from any original. Rubber stamps, tea-chests, old typewriters, and rusty signs have been used as inspiration and often even as original artwork. Scanners and digital cameras bring it to the desktop. Then it takes skill, talent, and serendipitous timing to turn an idea into a successful font. Just van Rossum and Erik van Blokland were the first type designers to get all the ingredients right when they grabbed everything looking like letters in their attic and scanned it. FF Karton, FF Confidential, and FF Trixie flaunt their simple analog heritage while being perfectly functional digital fonts.

A true trend came out of Berkeley, California. Zuzana Licko of Emigre Graphics was inspired by the primitive bitmap fonts generated by the first Macintosh computers. She designed her own types within those constraints. Now that bitmaps are back for technical reasons, those early designs show how much style can still be achieved.

Almost thirty years ago someone at International Typeface Corporation realized that people wanted "honest" typewriter faces, but with all the benefits of "real" type. Joel Kaden and Tony Stan designed ITC American Typewriter, which answers all those needs.

.HANDGLOVES
STENCIL

.HANDGLOVES
FF KARTON

.HANDGLOVES
FF CONFIDENTIAL

.Handgloves
EMIGRE TEN

.Handgloves
OAKLAND EIGHT

.Handgloves
ITC AMERICAN TYPEWRITER

If a note is scribbed quickly, chances are the letter shapes in the words will be connected. Every stop, start, and pen lift of the writing hand slows down the process. Neon signs and cursive fonts work hand in hand, so to speak.

Neon tubes are filled with gas; the more interruptions there are in the continuous loop, the more expensive it is to make the sign. Signmakers therefore have to look for typefaces that connect as many letters as possible, or they must manipulate other types to accommodate the technical constraints.

The neon-sign style, in turn, influenced graphic design, and people have spent a lot of time airbrushing a glow of light around curved, tubular letters. Like other graphic manipulations, achieving neon effects has become much easier with drawing and painting programs available on the computer.

Signmakers working with neon take pride in their ability to select any old typeface and reproduce it with glass tubes. Because neon messages are generally short, the signmaker will most likely take the entire word and make it into one shape. Even if inspiration comes from available type styles, the glass literally has to be bent and shaped to fit the design and technical requirements.

Since most signs are original designs, there hasn't been much call for real neon typefaces, although some fonts with glowing shadows and curvy shapes exist on transfer lettering. Some typefaces look as though they could be useful for neon signs. They have strokes of identical thickness throughout and no sharp angles or swelling of curves. Kaufmann fulfills these criteria and possesses some of that 1930s elegance.

The warm glow of the tube is created with the help of Adobe Photoshop.

Handgloves
KAUFMANN

Handgloves

Handgloves
FB NEON STREAM

Handgloves
HOUSE-A-RAMA LEAGUE NIGHT

Handgloves
LAS VEGAS FABULOUS

Handgloves
FB STREAMLINE

Handgloves
FB MAGNETO

We associate particular typeface looks with certain products. Fresh produce always seems to want an improvised, handwritten sort of message, while high-tech applications demand a cool, technocratic look. Warm, cuddly products respond to a soft serif treatment, grainy whole foods are represented best by a handmade, rough-edged typeface, and serious money businesses always recall the era of copperplate engraving, when assets were embodied in elaborately printed certificates.

In some cases this makes perfect sense. In produce and meat markets, where prices change constantly, time and expense prevent shopkeepers from having new signs printed each day. The most common solution is to write them out by hand; however, if the proprietor has illegible handwriting, it would be a disservice to customers to present an up-to-date but unreadable sign. The shopkeeper can simply buy a casual script or a brush font and print the signs reversed out on the laser printer. They will look almost like genuine handwriting on a blackboard.

Which one of these signs would you trust?

FRESH EGGS

Flying lessons

Fresh eggs

Flying lessons

Advertising, especially in newspapers, has always tried to emulate the spontaneous style of small-time shopkeepers and their signwriters. There were plenty of brushstroke typefaces available in hot metal days, even though the immediacy of brushstrokes and the rigidity of metal letters seem to be a contradiction. Many brushstroke typefaces now exist in digital form.

The names signal their potential applications: Brush Script and Reporter are the rough, brushstroke typefaces; Mistral, the most spontaneous design of them all, has already been praised in this book (see page 47).

With a little determination and a lot of software savvy, all of us today could make fonts. Some of these homemade fonts, sold by independent digital foundries, have recently become very popular. Among them are FF Erikrighthand, designed by Erik van Blokland, and FF Justlefthand by Just van Rossum, which began as practical jokes.

.*Handgloves*
BRUSH SCRIPT

.**Handgloves**
REPORTER

.*Handgloves*
MISTRAL

.*Handgloves*
FF MARKER-FAT

.Handgloves
FF PROVIDENCE

.Handgloves
FF ERIKRIGHTHAND

.Handgloves
FF JUSTLEFTHAND

FAX
Message

Frugal INC.
TIME MANAGEMENT

FRUGAL INC. TIME MANAGEMENT, 12 LATE STREET, KRONOS CITY, PM FAX 434 5369

To
The Timesavers/B. Franklin,
Savings Dept.
Cookoo's Clock-Street 9-5
Minnesota, 34 567 89,

From: Joe X. Ample

Date: 2.2.2002

No. of Pages

REGARDING Time Management

Dear Sirs,

Of all things we worked on lately, it appears that time was the most cost-intensive. Regarding that, we should not waste any of the company's precious resources. Fourty-five years of business experience indicate that wasted time is very hard to re-coup, as the statements at the end of the fiscal year always prove.

My proposal on this matter would be to intensify our efforts in the manufacturing field. We can not afford any delay; it would complicate the entire process. Instead, a hard-working industry would simplify many issues. Managers that arrive late in the morning will not be tolerated any longer. They hardly keep up with other, more efficient staff members.
It also shows that an inefficient and lengthy process costs more in time/money-terms than the actual manpower invested.

So what could be improved to avoid recession? We cannot make these times better if .... to wish for better times if we work hard m ... ...

FAX
Message

Frugal INC.
TIME MANAGEMENT

FRUGAL INC. TIME MANAGEMENT, 12 LATE STREET, KRONOS CITY, PM FAX 434 5369

From:
Joe X. Ample

Date: | 0 | 2 | 0 | 2 | 0 | 2 |

No. of Pages: | 0 | 3 |
(Including this one)

To:
The Timesavers/B. Frank
Savings Dept
Cookoo's Clock-Street 9-5
Minnesota, 34 567 89
Regarding:

Time Management

In Case of incomplete transmission
please call 1-800-F A X B A C K

Dear John

Of all things we worked on lately, it appears that time was the most cost-intensive. Regarding that, we should not waste any of the company's precious resources. Fourty-five years of business ... ... that wasted time is

Email notwithstanding, the letter is still the most common style of "formal" business communication. Letterheads make the first impression, and so are frequently printed on fine, heavy paper in several colors, sometimes with blind embossing or mock steel engraving.

Then what happens? The letter is followed by a proposal, a memo, or another letter. After the initial exchange, it seems appropriate to just send a fax. After this message has been subjected to the tortuous process of sending and receiving, color, nice paper, and beautiful, legible type become things of the past. No one in business could live without a fax machine anymore, but even a fax message should be good looking and legible.

For faxing, choose a sturdy, well-defined typeface (no delicate shapes here). The type has to withstand the rigors of the faxing procedure; this means it is scanned and then printed at a modest resolution of 200 dpi (dots per inch) after already having been distorted during transmission. Most types with a background in typewriter technology, Letter Gothic and Courier, for instance, don't work very well for faxing. Neither do those types we use for book settings, such as Caslon or Garamond, unless they're set in at least 14 point.

Other things to avoid are heavy lines and boxes (they get distorted); type smaller than 9 point; heavy rules to write on (they end up obscuring the very handwriting they are supposed to clarify); and type at the very bottom of the page (because it makes the machine scan all the way down to the bottom, even if you have only written a short message). Try using a few symbols to brighten things up: telephone icons, arrows to denote "to" and "from", a little house for the address, and hands or triangles as pointers or bullets.

.Handglov

LUCIDA TYPEWRITER

.Handgloves

LUCIDA SANS TYPEWRITER

.Handgloves

ITC STONE INFORMAL

.Handgloves

FF MAGDA CLEAN MONO

.Handgloves

PMN CAECILIA

.Handgloves

FF HARDCASE LIGHT CONDENSED

Frugal
INC.

MEMO Frugal Inc. Time Management, 12 Late Street, Kronos City,

The Timesavers/B.Frank
Savings Dept.
Cookoo's Clock-Street
Minnesota, 34567
www.the timesavers.c

DATE: 2. 2. 2002
TIME: 1:55 p.m.
TO: The Timesavers/B.Franklin
FROM: Joe X. Ample

Dear Sirs,

Of all the things we have worked on lately, it appears
as the most cost-intensive. Regarding that, we sh
of the company's precious resources. Forty-
experience indicate, that wasted tin
as the statements at the e

be to intensi
not affo

Frugal
Incorporated

Frugal Inc. Time Management, 12 Late Street, Kronos City, MN. 34567

MEMO:

TIME:
DATE: 2. 2. 2002
TO: 1:55 p.m.
FROM: The Timesavers/B.Franklin
Joe X. Ample

The Timesavers/B.Franklin,
Savings Dept.
Cookoo's Clock-Street 9-5
Minnesota, 34567
www.thetimesavers.com

Dear Sirs,

Of all the things we have worked on lately, it appears that time was the most
cost-intensive. Regarding that, we should not waste any of the company's
precious resources. Forty-five years of business experience indicate, that
wasted time is very difficult to re-coup , as the statements at the end of the
cal year invariably prove.
My proposal on this matter would be to intensify our efforts in the manu-
turing field . We cannot afford any delay; as it would complicate the entire
ress. Instead, a hard-working corporation would simplify many issues
gers who arrive late in the morning will not be tolera
hardly keep up with other, more efficient
o shows that ineffic
oney

Frugal
Incorporated

Time Management
12 Late Street
Kronos City, MN. 345678
here@thetimesavers.com
www.thetimesavers.com

The Timesavers/B.Franklin
Cookoo's Clock-Street 9-5
Kronos City, Minnesota 3456789

Memo

▷ The Timesavers/B.Franklin
◁ Joe X. Ample

Re-evaluating our progress

February 2. 2002
1:55 p.m.

Dear Sirs,

Of all the things we have worked on lately, it appears that time was the most cost-intensive. Regarding that, we should not waste any of the company's precious resources. Forty-five years of business experience indicate that wasted time is very difficult to re-coup, as the statements at the end of the fiscal year invariably prove.

My proposal on this matter would be to intensify our efforts in the manufacturing field . We cannot afford any delay; as it would complicate the entire process. Instead, a hard-working corporation would simplify many issues. Managers who arrive late in the morning will not be tolerated any longer; they hardly keep up with other, more efficient staff members. It also shows that inefficient and lengthy processes cost more in time/money-terms than the actual manpower invested.

So what could be improved to avoid recession? We cannot make these times better if we ignore our responsibility.

Regarding our meeting scheduled for next Wednesday the 4th, please bring your new product for our time analysts to review.

Most of what's been said about faxes also applies to memos. However, because memos are not normally subjected to scanning and transmission over a wire, you can use type that is more delicate. In fact, most typefaces used for books, newspapers, and magazines look fine when printed on a good laser printer, as long as the type is not too small.

You might want to get across that "old" office feel of the typewriter and its no-nonsense look. Try any of the sturdy-serif fonts – Corona, Glypha, Egyptienne F – or choose a cool matter-of-fact typeface like FF Info Office, Bell Gothic, or ITC Officina Serif. If you're looking for a traditional look, use Proforma, ITC Charter, or Utopia.

The rules of legibility also apply to memos. Make sure your lines are fairly short (the optimum is ten words), and put a narrow column next to the main message for headings and identification. The first things your correspondent should see are: who the memo is *to*, who it is *from*, *what* it is about, and *when* it was written.

. Handgloves
CORONA

. Handgloves
GLYPHA

. Handgloves
EGYPTIENNE F

. **Handgloves**
FF INFO OFFICE BOLD

. Handgloves
BELL GOTHIC BOLD

. Handgloves
ITC OFFICINA SERIF MEDIUM

. Handgloves
PROFORMA BOOK

. Handgloves
ITC CHARTER

. Handgloves
UTOPIA

. Handgloves
FOUNDRY FORM SERIF

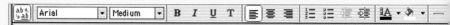

Billions of e-mails are sent every day, more than letters, faxes and memos together. An e-mail combines the advantage of a phone call with t[...] but provides proof of what has been said. Or so it should be. Netiquette, however, is not followed by everybody, which means that e-mails of[...] legible than letters.

The first thing to avoid is html formatting. This is the standard for text on the World Wide Web, but e-mail programs that cannot read html will [...] Which means that the text could run as wide as the window with lines as long as 300 characters. Legible lines should be shorter than 75 char[...] automatically wrap lines at around that mark. Plain text messages contain no formatting in the first place, so you can be sure that it'll look the[...] can only be composed and read in mono-spaced fonts, the lines will break the same as in the original.

The second big issue concerns the reply button. Any phrase you highlight in your mail will automatically by repeated in your response. But ev[...] sentence from someone else's e-mail, you don't need to send it all back. Hit the reply button, then place your answer underneath the text you[...] snail mail correspondents send your original letter back with their response? A little concern for the recipient of your messages goes a long w[...]

Billions of e-mails are sent every day, more than letters, faxes and memos together. An e-mail combines the advantage of a phone call with those of written communication: it is short and immediate, but provides proof of what has been said. Or so it should be. Netiquette, however, is not followed by everybody, which means that e-mails often turn out to be longer than phone calls and less legible than letters.

The first thing to avoid is html formatting. This is the standard for text on the World Wide Web, but e-mail programs that cannot read html will most likely display the message as unformatted text. Which means that the text could run as wide as the window with lines as long as 300 characters. Legible lines should be shorter than 75 characters, and many e-mail applications actually automatically wrap lines at around that mark. Plain text messages contain no formatting in the first place, so you can be sure that it'll look the same to the recipient as it does to you. And as they can only be composed and read in mono-spaced fonts, the lines will break the same as in the original.

The second big issue concerns the reply button. Any phrase you highlight in your mail will automatically by repeated in your response. But even if you want to quote more than one contiguous sentence from someone else's e-mail, you don't need to send it all back. Hit the reply button, then place your answer underneath the text you're referring to and delete all the other stuff. Or do your snail mail correspondents send your original letter back with their response? A little concern for the recipient of your messages goes a long way.

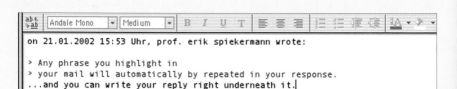

on 21.01.2002 15:53 Uhr, prof. erik spiekermann wrote:

> Any phrase you highlight in
> your mail will automatically by repeated in your response.
...and you can write your reply right underneath it.

Billions of emails are sent every day, more than letters, faxes, and memos together. An email combines the advantages of a phone call with those of written communication: it is short and immediate, but provides proof of what has been said. Or so it should be. Netiquette, however, is not followed by everybody, which means that emails often turn out to be longer than phone calls and less legible than letters. The first thing to avoid is HTML formatting. This is the standard for text on the World Wide Web, but email programs that cannot read HTML will most likely display the message as unformatted text. This means that the text could run as wide as the window and have lines as long as 300 characters. Legible lines should be shorter than 75 characters, and many email applications automatically wrap lines at around that mark. Plain text messages contain no formatting in the first place, so you can be sure that it'll look the same to the recipient as it does to you. And because plain text can only be composed and read in monospaced fonts, the lines will break the same as in the original.

The second big issue concerns the reply button. Any phrase you highlight in your mail automatically is repeated in your response. But even if you want to quote more than one contiguous sentence from someone else's email, you don't need to send it all back. Hit the reply button, then place your answer underneath the text you're referring to and delete all the other stuff. Or do your snail mail correspondents send your original letter back with their response? A little consideration for the recipient of your messages goes a long way.

Top example shows what an email can look like with HTML formatting. The better the screen resolution, the smaller the type. The second illustration is the text from this column set in Andale Mono, 12 point, which seems to be the minimum size to avoid damage to your eyes. Underneath the phrase to be quoted in the reply, and at the bottom the reply, short and sweet.

For a bit of typographic choice, you could pick something other than Courier – for example Andale Mono. Even if the recipients don't have as much typographic taste as you do, the format you send will be almost exactly what they get.

Apart from consideration for the recipient and typographic vanity, we also need to be concerned with legibility of emails on our own screens.

At the recommended 12 point, differences between monospaced fonts can be quite explicit.

Handgloves12
Handgloves12

Even good old Courier exists in more than one version. Check your system fonts.

Handgloves12
Handgloves12

Andale Mono and Lucida Typewriter also come free with some programs.

Handgloves12
Handgloves12
Handgloves12
Handgloves12
Handgloves12
Handgloves12
Handgloves12
Handgloves12

If you want fine increments in weight, you have a look at Thesis Monospace. And there isn't even room to show the corresponding italics ...

Expense Schedule

	1	2				
NTH						
LARIES	8000	8500				1050
INGE BENEFITS AND TAXES	2300	2300				230
NT	4600	0				160
SURANCE						
AVELING	900	900	900	900	900	90
EIGHT/MAI	200	200	200	200	200	20
PAIR	100	100	100	100	100	10
ASING MACH	0					
LEPHONE	500					
FICE SUPPLI	3000					
URNALS	100					
GAL AND AC	5000					
NK CHARGES	50					
OTOCOPIES	0					
TOMOBILES	0					
VERTISING	3000					
NSULTING	0					
HER	100					
CURITY	600					
M	28950					

Financial Statement
December 31, 2001

Assets		
Current Assets		
Cash	1,000	
Accounts Receivable	3,000	
Notes Receivable	1,500	
Merchandise Inventory		40,000
Office Supplies		
Store Supplies		
Prepaid Insurance		
Total Current Assets		46,500
Plant Assets		
Land	5,000	
Buildings		76,000
Less Accumulated Depreciation	3,000	73,000
Store Equipment		20,000
Less Accumulated Depreciation	6,000	14,000
Total Plant Assets		92,000
Investments		50,000
Patents		10,000
Good Will	5,000	

NEWS GOTHIC

Financial Statement
December 31, 2005

Assets
Current Assets

Cash	21,456		
Accounts Receivable	33,789		
Notes Receivable	31,012		
Merchandise Inventory		240,234	
Office Supplies	41,345		
Store Supplies	52,678		
Prepaid Insurance		323,567	
Current Assets		446,890	
Plant Assets			
Land	65,902		
Buildings			276,123
Less Accumulated		345,567	
Depreciation	73,234	273,456	
Store Equipment			320,789
Less Accumulated	23,456		

MINION CONDENSED

Financial Statement
December 31, 2005

Assets
Current Assets

Cash	21,456		
Accounts Receivable	33,789		
Notes Receivable	31,012		
Merchandise Inventory		240,234	
Office Supplies	41,345		
Store Supplies	52,678		
Prepaid Insurance		323,567	
Current Assets		446,890	
Plant Assets			
Land	65,902		
Buildings			276,123
Less Accumulated		345,567	
Depreciation	73,234	273,456	
Store Equipment			320,789
Less Accumulated	23,456		

UNIVERS 57

Financial Statement
December 31, 2005

Assets
Current Assets

Cash	21,456		
Accounts Receivable	33,789		
Notes Receivable	31,012		
Merchandise Inventory		240,234	
Office Supplies	41,345		
Store Supplies	52,678		
Prepaid Insurance		323,567	
Current Assets		446,890	
Plant Assets			
Land	65,902		
Buildings			276,123
Less Accumulated		345,456	
Depreciation	73,234	273,456	
Store Equipment			320,789
Less Accumulated			
Depreciation		436,123	414,345
Plant Assets	34,345	945,234	

Spreadsheets – as the name implies – need plenty of space. If you set them in Courier, you will end up with type that is small, and very easy to misread.

There are numerals that save space and that are still more legible than Helvetica or Times or those in your standard word-processor font. Figures in tables have to be the same width or they will not line up properly in columns. Lining figures (numerals that don't have ascenders and descenders) are usually tabular, and so do a reasonable job in this situation; lining figures are standard in most modern digital fonts.

For maximum legibility with added space economy, look at narrower-than-normal typefaces like News Gothic, or at condensed versions like Univers 57, Minion Condensed, and Frutiger Condensed. These types will set your spreadsheets apart from the norm: not only will they look better, but they will read better.

• 1234567890
NEWS GOTHIC

• 1234567890
UNIVERS 57

• 1234567890
MINION MM CONDENSED

• 1234567890
FRUTIGER CONDENSED

• 1234567890
FF INFO OFFICE

• 1234567890
FF META

• 1234567890
ITC OFFICINA

Normal-Mas

Otto Parcus

Quirin Reiner

Südfrüchte &
Thee.

Ulrich Vormun

Wilhelm Xaver Zeitb

No matter what turns technology takes, the typefaces we see most will still be those based upon letterforms from the end of the fifteenth century; the original Venetian or German models are evident in the diverse interpretations of every type designer since then. Garamond, Caslon, Baskerville, Bodoni; Gill, Zapf, Dwiggins, Frutiger: they all found inspiration in the past for typeface designs that were appropriate for their times and their tools. Every new imaging technology (as we call it today) results in a new generation of type designs. Today, outline fonts can emulate any shape imaginable, if not necessarily desirable; they can equal and even improve upon every aesthetic and technical refinement ever dreamed of or achieved.

This was new, modern, beautiful type in 1886. Later generations called the nineteenth century the "worst period in typographic history"; today we again admire the nostalgic charm of these decorative typefaces.

Apart from the typefaces that work well because we are familiar with them, there are those that defy the simplistic classifications of usefulness or purpose. They may exist only because the type designer's first thought one morning was a new letter shape. These private artistic expressions may not appeal to a wide audience, but every now and again the right singer effortlessly transforms a simple song into a great hit. There are typographic gems hidden in today's specimen books just waiting to be discovered. In the right hands, technical constraints turn into celebrations of simplicity, and awkward alphabets are typographic heroes for a day.

There is no bad type.

It takes time for a typeface to progress from concept through production to distribution, and from there to the type user's awareness. Typefaces are indicators of our visual and thus, cultural climate; type designers, therefore, have to be good at anticipating future trends. No amount of marketing will get a typeface accepted if it runs against the spirit of the time.

Every once in a while a typeface is revived by graphic designers and typographers who dust it off and display it in new environments either as a reaction against prevailing preferences or simply because they want to try something different. Actual problem-solving often seems not to matter when it comes to choosing typefaces. True classic typefaces – that is, those with the beauty and proportion of their fifteenth-century ancestors – still win awards in the most chic and modern design annuals.

There is no bad type.

When you get to the fork
in the road, take it.

Yogi Berra (1925–), Hall-of-
Fame catcher for the New York
Yankees, was one of the great
all-time clutch hitters and a
notorious bad ball hitter.
Berra, who later managed the
Yankees, has a natural ability
to turn ordinary thoughts into
linguistic ringers.

CHAPTER 10

Final Form

Bibliography

Learning to use type properly might take a lifetime, but it will be a lifetime of fun. In case you have now been bitten by the typographic bug, here is what we recommend as further reading on the subject. The list is far from complete, but includes both practical manuals and classic works. Some of these books are out of print, but can be found with a little effort in good used book stores or online.

Not that we suggest you do your reading online, but plenty of useful information about type & typography can be found on the web.

BIGELOW, CHARLES, PAUL HAYDEN DUENSING, LINNEA GENTRY. *Fine Print On Type: The Best of Fine Print on Type and Typography.* San Francisco: Fine Print/Bedford Arts, 1988.

BLUMENTHAL, JOSEPH. *The Printed Book in America.* Boston: David R. Godine, 1977.

BRANCZYK, ALEXANDER, JUTTA NACHTWEY, HEIKE NEHL, SIBYLLE SCHLAICH, JÜRGEN SIEBERT, EDS. *Emotional Digital: A Sourcebook of Contemporary Typographics.* New York and London: Thames and Hudson, 2001

BRINGHURST, ROBERT. *The Elements of Typographic Style. 2nd ed.* Point Roberts, Washington: Hartley & Marks, 1997.

CARTER, SEBASTIAN. *Twentieth Century Type Designers.* New York: W.W. Norton & Company, 1999.

CHAPPELL, WARREN, with ROBERT BRINGHURST. *A Short History of the Printed Word.* Point Roberts, Washington: Hartley & Marks, 2000.

The Chicago Manual of Style. 15th Edition. Chicago: The University of Chicago Press, 2002.

DAIR, CARL. *Design with Type.* Toronto and Buffalo: University of Toronto Press, 1982.

DOWDING, GEOFFREY. *Finer Points in the Spacing and Arrangement of Type.* Point Roberts, Washington: Hartley & Marks, 1998.

DOWDING, GEOFFREY. *An Introduction to the History of Printing Types.* London: The British Library, 1997.

DRUCKER, JOHANNA. *The Alphabetic Labyrinth, the Letters in History and Imagination.* London: Thames and Hudson, 1997.

DWIGGINS, WILLIAM ADDISON. *Layout in Advertising.* New York: Harper and Brothers, 1948.

FRUTIGER, ADRIAN. *Type, Sign, Symbol.* Zurich: ABC Verlag, 1980.

GILL, ERIC. *An Essay on Typography.* Boston: David R. Godine, 1988.

GORDON, BOB. *Making Digital Type Look Good.* New York:Watson-Guptill, 2001.

GRAY, NICOLETE. *A History of Lettering: Creative Experiment and Letter Identity.* Boston: David R. Godine, 1986.

HARLING, ROBERT. *The Letter Forms and Type Designs of Eric Gill.* Boston: David R. Godine, 1977.

Hart's Rules for Compositors and Readers. London: Oxford University Press, 1967.

HLAVSA, OLDŘICH. *A Book of Type and Design.* New York: Tudor Publishing, 1960.

JASPERT, W. PINCUS, W. TURNER BERRY, A.F. JOHNSON. *The Encyclopedia of Type Faces.* New York: Blandford Press, 1986.

JOHNSTON, ALASTAIR. *Alphabets to Order: The Literature of Nineteenth-Century Typefounders' Specimens.* London: The British Library; New Castle, Delaware: Oak Knoll, 2000.

KELLY, ROB ROY. *American Wood Type 1828–1900.* New York: Van Nostrand Reinhold, 1969.

KINROSS, ROBIN. *Anthony Froshaug: Typography & Texts / Documents of a Life.* Princeton: Princeton Architectural Press, 2001.

KINROSS, ROBIN. *Modern Typography: An Essay in Critical History.* London: Hyphen Press, 1992.

LAWSON, ALEXANDER. *Anatomy of a Typeface.* Boston: David R. Godine, 1990.

LAWSON, ALEXANDER. *Printing Types: An Introduction.* Boston: Beacon Press, 1971.

LEWIS, JOHN. *Anatomy of Printing: The Influence of Art and History on Its Design.* New York: Watson Guptill, 1970.

McGREW, MAC. *American Metal Typefaces of the Twentieth Century.* New Castle, Delaware: Oak Knoll, 1993.

McLEAN, RUARI. *How Typography Happens.* London: The British Library; New Castle, Delaware: Oak Knoll, 2000.

McLEAN, RUARI. *Jan Tschichold: Typographer.* Boston: David R. Godine, 1975.

McLEAN, RUARI. *The Thames and Hudson Manual of Typography.* London and New York: Thames and Hudson, 1980.

MEGGS, PHILIP B, ROY McKELVEY, EDS. *Revival of the Fittest: Digital Versions of Classic Typefaces.* Cincinnati, Ohio: North Light Books, 2000.

MERRIMAN, FRANK. A.T.A. *Type Comparison Book.* New York: Advertising Typographers Association of America, 1965.

MORISON, STANLEY. *First Principles of Typography.* New York: The Macmillan Company, 1936.

MORISON, STANLEY. *A Tally of Types.* Boston: David R. Godine, 1999.

PIPES, ALAN. *Production for Graphic Designers.* 3rd ed. New York The Overlook Press, 2001.

ROGERS, BRUCE. *Paragraphs on Printing.* New York: Dover Publications, 1979.

SPIEKERMANN, ERIK. *Rhyme & Reason: A Typographical Novel.* Berlin: Berthold, 1987.

TRACY, WALTER. *Letters of Credit: A View of Type Design.* London: Gordon Fraser, 1986.

TSCHICHOLD, JAN. *Alphabets and Lettering: A Source Book of the Best Letter Forms of Past and Present for Sign Painters, Graphic Artists, Typographers, Printers, Sculptors, Architects, and Schools of Art and Design.* Ware, Hertfordshire, England: Omega Books, 1985.

TSCHICHOLD, JAN. *The Form of the Book: Essays on the Morality of Good Design.* Point Roberts, Washington: Hartley & Marks, 1997.

UPDIKE, DANIEL BERKELEY. *Printing Types: Their History, Forms, and Use.* 2 vols. New Castle, Delaware: Oak Knoll, 2001.

WILLIAMSON, HUGH. *Methods of Book Design: The Practice of an Industrial Craft.* New Haven and London: Yale University Press, 1985.

Index

Typeface index

Credits

8 Paul Watzlawick

Quotation is
public domain

28 *Hypnerotomachia
Poliphili*

Photo:
Fred Brady

10 Salt & pepper

Photo:
Dennis Hearne,
San Francisco

30 Handwriting samples

From the library of
Jack Stauffacher,
San Francisco

12 Newspapers

Photo:
© Good Shoot
Business and
Communication

32 Winter tree

Photo:
Peter de Lory,
San Francisco

16 Labels

Typographic design:
Thomas Nagel

34 www

Typographic design:
Michael Balgavy,
Vienna

20 Egg

Photo:
Erik Spiekermann,
Berlin

36 Sigmund Freud

Quotation attributed
to Mr. Freud

22 German
freeway sign

Photo:
Helmuth Langer,
Köln

40-42 Shoes

Photo:
© Adobe Systems

Cover design:
Susanna Dulkinys and
Erik Spiekermann
San Francisco

Sheep drawing
courtesy of
csaimages.com

24 Tallulah Bankhead

Quotation attributed
to Ms. Bankhead

44 Doubt

Photo:
Dennis Hearne,
San Francisco
Model:
Megan Biermann

6 Street sign,
Stockholm

Photo:
Erik Spiekermann,
Berlin

26 Trajan Column,
Rome

Photo: Victoria &
Albert Museum,
London

46 Surprise

Photo:
Dennis Hearne,
San Francisco
Model:
Megan Biermann

48 Joy

Photo:
Dennis Hearne,
San Francisco
Model:
Megan Biermann

50 Anger

Photo:
Dennis Hearne,
San Francisco
Model:
Megan Biermann

54 Hand drawing
Leonardo da Vinci

Photo:
© Visual Language Library
Art of Anatomy (VIII)

56 Palm Pilot

Photo:
Erik Spiekermann,
Berlin

58 Gerry Mulligan

Quotation from a
radio interview:
used with permission
of National Public Radio

60 Packing to travel

Photo:
Peter de Lory,
San Francisco

62 Vacation

Photo:
Peter de Lory,
San Francisco

64 Business

Photo:
Peter de Lory,
San Francisco

66 Work

Photo:
Peter de Lory,
San Francisco

68 Formal

Photo:
Peter de Lory,
San Francisco

70 Trendy

Photo:
Peter de Lory,
San Francisco

72 Mosaic facade

Photo:
Erik Spiekermann,
San Francisco

74 Sherlock Holmes

Quotation from
Beatrice Warde used
with permission of the
Typophiles, inc.

94 Symbols

Typographic design:
Thomas Nagel

96 Eric Gill

Quotation used
with permission
of David R. Godine,
Publishers

98, 100, 102
John, Paul, George & Rita

Photos:
Dennis Hearne,
San Francisco

104 The Trapp family

Photo:
© Wide World Photo

106 Guitars

Photo:
© Wide World Photo

108 The Lawrence Welk
family

Photo:
© The Bettman Archives

110 The Concert (ca. 1550)

© The Bridgeman
Art Library

112 Tuba player

Photo:
© Wide World Photo

114 Metronome

Photo:
Dennis Hearne,
San Francisco

116 Young Philharmonic
Orchestra, Vienna

Photo:
Rita Newman,
Vienna

118 Small book

Photo:
Dennis Hearne,
San Francisco
from the collection
of Joyce Lancaster
Wilson

120 Anti-aliasing

Photo:
Ralf Weissmantel,
Berlin

122 Frederic Goudy

Quotation attributed
to Mr. Goudy

124 Tree plantation

Photo:
© Science Photo Library
Contrast, Vienna

126 Summer tree

Photo:
Peter de Lory,
San Francisco

128 Marathon
runners

Photo:
© Tony Stone Images
David Madison

130 Sprinter

Photo:
© Buenos Dias
Stock Directory
Spencer Rowell

132 Freeway day
& night

Photo:
© Transglobe Vienna,
Contrast
Uselmann, Fauner

134 Traffic lanes

Photo:
Photo Alto,
Roads and Bridges
Frédérik Cirou

136 City traffic

Photo:
© Corbis Stock Market
David Sailors 2002

138 Traffic jam

Photo:
Photo Alto,
Paris the city
Isabelle Rozenbaum,
Frédérik Cirou

139 Noise

Typographic design:
Michael Balgavy,
Vienna

142 William
Addison Dwiggins

Quote used with
permission of Harper
Collins, Publishers

144 Bedroom

Photo:
Dennis Hearne,
San Francisco

146 Living room

Photo:
M. Helfer/
Superstock

148 Hotel lobby

Photo:
Hotel Triton,
San Francisco;
Dennis Hearne,
San Francisco

150 Kitchen

Photo:
M. Helfer/
Superstock

152 Typing pool

Photo:
© Historical Pictures/
Stock Montage

154 Razorfish Studio
San Francisco

Photo:
Erik Spiekermann,
San Francisco

156 Groucho Marx

Quotation used
with permission
of Simon & Schuster,
Publishers

158 Stencils

Photo:
Erik Spiekermann,
Berlin

160 Neon sign

Photo:
Peter de Lory,
San Francisco!

162 Shop signs,
Paris

Photo:
Erik Spiekermann,
Berlin

172 Type specimen

Reproduced with permission
from *Typology*,
by Steven Heller
and Louise Fili.
Chronicle Books, SF

174 Yogi Berra

Quotation attributed
to Mr. Berra

E.M. Ginger

has worked with fine books, type, and typography for three decades in the capacities of author, editor, typographer, reviewer, designer, instructor, critic, and weekend printer. She began her book training at The Stinehour Press, a letterpress printer/publisher of fine books, multi-disciplined scholarly journals, and catalogues of rare book and fine art collections; there, she began her life-long love of printing history, learned the workings of the Monotype typesetting system, and handset and printed foundry types.

She was managing editor (and occasional production manager and design director) of *Fine Print: The Review for the Arts of the Book* for twelve years. A letterpress-printed journal of well-crafted critical reviews of fine press books and reference works, Fine Print covered technical and creative innovations relating to the history and arts of the book including type design, papermaking, bookbinding, calligraphy, printing, illustration technique, and bibliography. At Adobe Systems, she worked in the Adobe Originals Type Group as a manager, writer, instructor, and printing and type historian.

Ms. Ginger is currently the executive editor at Octavo, a company that publishes and produces digital rare books; she selects the books to be published and interprets their editorial, design, illustrative, and typographic requirements into digital formats. She is the editor of several award-winning cookbooks and books on type, typography, and design.

Erik Spiekermann

Born in 1947 near Hanover, Germany, Erik Spiekermann calls himself a typographic designer as well as a type designer. He financed his Art History studies at Berlin's Free University by running a printing press and setting metal type in the basement of his house. After seven years as a freelance designer in London, he returned to Berlin in 1979. There he founded MetaDesign, which grew into Germany's largest design firm, with more than 200 staff by the year 2000.

MetaDesign's San Francisco office opened in 1992 with partners Bill Hill and Terry Irwin, and a London office was opened in 1995. Worldwide clients ranged from Adobe Systems, Apple Computer, Audi, Berlin Transit, Dusseldorf International Airport, IBM and Nike to Skoda, Lexus Europe, Heidelberg Printing Machines and Volkswagen.

Erik began his type design career by redrawing old hot metal faces from the Berthold library, back in the 70s: LoType and Berliner Grotesk. In 1989, Erik founded FontShop International, publishers of the FontFont library. The library includes several of his own designs. FF Meta has become one of the most popular typefaces in the USA and Europe. Another of his typefaces, ITC Officina, is widely used in Web design. FF Info, his latest effort, has been chosen for the navigation system of a major European airport.

Erik has written numerous articles and four books about type and typography, including *Stop Stealing Sheep* for Adobe Press.

He is a member of the board of directors of the AtypI; a member of the Type Directors Club New York, The Art Directors Club, AIGA, ACD, and D&AD, and many more. He is a Fellow of the International Society of Typographic Designers UK, Vice-President of the German Design Council, President of the International Institute for Information Design, and an honorary member of the Typographic Circle London. He holds an honorary professorship at the Academy of Arts in Bremen, and teaches workshops at design schools across the world. His entertaining lectures and oft-controversial participation as a competition judge have earned him an international reputation as one of Germany's leading communication designers.

Erik's work has been credited as offering a blend of Teutonic efficiency and an Anglos-Saxon sense of humor. In July 2000, Erik withdrew from the management of MetaDesign Berlin. He now works as a freelance design consultant in Berlin, London and San Francisco. He has since redesigned THE ECONOMIST magazine in London as well as REASON magazine in the US and a new corporate typeface for NOKIA CORP.

Design
First edition: MetaDesign West, San Francisco,
California; update: Erik Spiekermann

Typesetting, illustration research, and page production
Susanne Dechant, Susanna Dulkinys,
Magdalena Duftner, Ernestine Janich-Böhm,
Carmen Leitner, Sandra Walti

Readers and type advisors
Jocelyn Bergen, Elsie V. Brenner, Margery
Cantor, Burwell Davis, Molly S. Detwiler,
Ilene N. Ellickson, Lynne Garell, Alexander
Lawson, Mac McGrew, Will H. Powers,
Fritz Streiff, Carol Twombly

Editors
E.M. Ginger & Kelly Ryer

Production coordinator
Kate Reber

Cover design
Susanna Dulkinys and Erik Spiekermann

Primary text fonts are Myriad and Minion.
Additional typefaces were supplied by FontShop
International (FontFont library), FontBureau,
House Industries, Emigré, Gerard Unger, and
ITC International Typeface Corporation.

Sheep drawing courtesy of Chuck Anderson,
csaimages.com
Printed by CDS Publications in Medford, Oregon.